I SEE BLACK PEOP

ALSO BY KRISTAL BRENT ZOOK

Color by Fox: The Fox Network and the Revolution in Black Television

Black Women's Lives: Stories of Power and Pain

I SEE BLACK PEOPLE

THE RISE AND FALL OF AFRICAN AMERICAN–OWNED TELEVISION AND RADIO

KRISTAL BRENT ZOOK

NATION
BOOKS

Published by Nation Books
A Member of the Perseus Books Group
116 East 16th Street, 8th Floor
New York, NY 10003

Nation Books is a co-publishing venture of the Nation Institute
and the Perseus Books Group

Books published by Nation Books are available at special discounts for
bulk purchases in the United States by corporations, institutions, and
other organizations. For more information, please contact the Special
Markets Department at the Perseus Books Group, 2300 Chestnut Street,
Suite 200, Philadelphia, PA 19103, or call (800) 255-1514, or e-mail
special.markets@perseusbooks.com.

Interior design by Cynthia Young. Set in Adobe Caslon.

Library of Congress Cataloging-in-Publication Data

Zook, Kristal Brent.
I see black people : the rise and fall of African American–owned
television and radio / Kristal Brent Zook.
p. cm.
ISBN–13: 978-1-56025-999-2 (alk. paper)
ISBN–10: 156025999X
1. Television stations—United States—Management.   2. Radio
stations—United States—Management.   3. African Americans in
television broadcasting.   4. African Americans in radio broadcasting.
5. African American businesspeople—Biography.   I. Title.
HE8689.8.Z66 2008
384.54092'396073—dc22
2007039612

10 9 8 7 6 5 4 3 2 1

CONTENTS

INTRODUCTION

When a journalist goes to interview a stranger, there are, at times, moments of discomfort. One such moment happened for me about fifteen years ago. Inside a shiny new office building at the corner of Slauson and La Cienega boulevards in South Los Angeles, I met with Eugene and Phyllis Jackson, the founders of an aspiring new cable venture called The World African Network (WAN). A premium channel, WAN was to be dedicated to the "cultural uplift of African descendants."

The Jacksons, an elegant couple, struck me as genuine people who believed deeply in their mission. I liked them. At the same time, there was a subtle tension in the air (at least I felt it) as I surveyed the Kente cloth–wearing staff members and the Afrocentric decor splashed throughout the offices. Their plan for content, they said, was to air only "culturally correct" programming from the African Diaspora. To ensure this correctness, they would institute a measuring system, an "Africanity index," as they put it, that would gauge appropriate levels of blackness.

It was then that I, a biracial African American, knew that the Jacksons would not succeed in their attempt to reach "all of us." How could they when the red flag of "authentic blackness" had been raised, promising to exclude anyone who did not fit the mold?

I watched as WAN tried for years to secure distribution, and ultimately failed. The Jacksons moved their headquarters to Atlanta and then quietly disappeared from the media radar. I'm told by those in a position to know that Eugene Jackson now lives in South Africa where he raises pigs and sheep and has several successful business ventures.

Over many years of writing about television and media ownership, I have come across dozens of similar stories. African Americans have had great hopes for starting broadcast and cable ventures. African Americans have had great hopes for starting broadcast and cable ventures, and yet very few have succeeded. WAN even had support from superstar Janet Jackson (no relation to Phyllis or Eugene), and yet very few have succeeded.

Within these business plans are troubling perceptions about what African American audiences want. What do we dream about, and how does our media consumption fuel or thwart our desires? So many of those who have attempted to capture our attention have been wrong about the answers to these questions. What some programmers think black people might like to watch is often a far cry from what black people do, in fact, spend their time watching.

This point hit home again when I decided to look into the 2004 launch of TV One for *The New York Times Sunday Magazine*. In that essay, I described the scene at an intimate gathering of friends in an upscale Murray Hill apartment in Manhattan. The crowd included our host, an

African American financial entrepreneur with an MBA from Harvard; an African American Syrian who was raised by white adoptive parents in the Midwest; a Caucasian auctioneer with Christie's; an Iranian money manager, and the list went on. Most of the friends were black with varying ties to the Diaspora.

Here is what struck me. At exactly 7 p.m. on this Sunday evening, the music was unexpectedly turned down and the television turned on. The group watched quietly, fully engaged, the stories on *60 Minutes* about oil wealth in Equatorial Guinea and about a rural community in Virginia where residents still used outhouses.

Once again, it seemed to me that those who assumed that black folks preferred gum-smacking, jive-talking sitcoms were proven wrong. Still, a 2000 Screen Actors Guild study showed that nearly 45 percent of African American primetime characters on broadcast television remain confined to urban sitcoms. But just as programmers at WAN were wrong about restricting us to a nationalistic rhetoric of cultural pride and ethnocentricity, the folks at TV One were also missing the mark when it came to our vastly divergent tastes and preferences. In fact, as I discovered in subsequent research, *60 Minutes* ranked eighteenth among upper-income African Americans, the initial target audience of the new network. (In contrast, among the total American market ages eighteen to forty-nine it fell to a low forty-first place.)

I was convinced that there was a striking disconnect between what some black audiences wanted and what we were actually getting. I wondered how black ownership changed things. How did these radio and television stations envision their audiences? I wanted to talk to some of them, but there was a problem: Where were they?

African Americans are disproportionately high television viewers—watching 44 percent more network television than non-blacks. But those who decide what these environments will look like are, by and large, not black. Total minority media ownership of television and radio is currently about 3 percent, and falling. African Americans own less than 1 percent of all television stations in the country. The airwaves are public resources; they belong to the people. And yet only a small fraction of them are owned and controlled by people of color. How did we get here?

During the 1970s, in the midst of the civil rights movement and a growing awareness of injustice in all forms, the American public forced the issue of media ownership to the forefront of our nation's consciousness. Some leaders agreed that there was a problem and began to address it. In 1976 the U.S. Court of Appeals told the Federal Communications Commission that it was mistaken in not considering a person's race on applications for broadcast station ownership. The court further advised the FCC—the government agency responsible for regulating radio, television, wire, satellite, and cable communication—that it should begin to include race as a factor in deciding which applicants to grant licenses to, as a way to begin to rectify such grave historical imbalances. As a result of this landmark decision, the FCC developed its groundbreaking Minority

Ownership Policy. During the policy's more than fifteen-year existence, it succeeded in helping minority ownership to inch slowly upward.

Dorothy Brunson was both the first African American woman ever to own a radio station in America and one of the first African American woman to own a television station. In 1969, prior to these ventures, she was also cofounder of the first black-owned advertising agency on Madison Avenue, which launched with $25,000 in Small Business Administration loans. Her story is here in this book.

So are the thoughts and perspectives of Pierre and Percy Sutton, who founded Inner City Broadcasting in 1972, then the largest black-owned group of radio stations in the country. "For thirty years," Percy Sutton recently told members of the press, "One of the company's radio stations WLIB has been geared to the black community, and not one year have we been able to make it break even."

Radio One, founded by Catherine Liggins Hughes—the first African American woman to head a firm publicly traded on the U.S. Stock Exchange—is behind the largest black-oriented radio network in the country. Hughes bought her first station in 1980, WOL-AM 1450 in Washington, DC. Today Radio One is valued at more than $3 billion.

In January of 2004, Radio One launched TV One, in partnership with Comcast, the largest cable operator in the country. The network (which uses the slogan "I See Black People" in its advertising) is now in more than

40 million households, or about half the number of Black Entertainment Television (BET) homes. I spoke with Cathy Hughes about her legendary contributions to the black-owned media landscape.

The story of Robert Short, his family, and members of his church and community, are also here. Short is the former owner of WRDS-FM, the first black-owned radio station in Syracuse, New York. He sold his station, reluctantly, in 2000. His experience offers compelling evidence of how the loss of one station can impact an entire community.

Booker Wade is general manager of KMTP in San Francisco, California, one of only two African American–owned public television stations in the country. His story begins in the early 1980s, when he was a Washington, DC-based lawyer with the FCC. In those early days, he forged a business partnership with actor and "singing cowboy" Gene Autry, and was well on his way to owning the first black cable network. Although the venture was well-conceived and financed, it failed. I wanted to know why. Wade, who continues his long struggle to bring diversity to the airwaves at KMTP, provided fascinating answers to my questions.

Jim Winston is executive director of the National Association of Black-Owned Broadcasters and one of the FCC lawyers who invested with Booker Wade in 1980. In his 2003 testimony before the FCC, Winston stated that minority media ownership had plummeted by 14 percent since the passage of the Telecommunications Act of 1996.

His perspective is also here, based on decades of advocating for African American and other minority owners.

Frank Washington is a critical player in the story of minority media ownership. In fact, he refers to himself as both the "alpha and omega" of the FCC's Minority Ownership Policy. After playing a major role in initiating the original legislation from the 1970s, Washington also helped to bring these policies down with one deal gone bad, twenty years later.

Willie Davis, a former NFL Super Bowl champion for the Green Bay Packers, was unlike most athletes of his day. Not only did he play in the country's first two Super Bowls, but he also had the foresight to plan for a life after sports. His teammates teased him when he went back to school to earn his MBA from the University of Chicago. But after retiring in 1969, he founded All Pro Broadcasting, Inc., which today remains a majority black-owned company. Davis owns four radio stations in California and Wisconsin. His story is also here.

Not long after WVON-AM (then known as the "Voice of the Negro") went on the air in 1963, it became an institution in the city of Chicago with profound political and social power. Today, Melody Spann-Cooper, the forty-two-year-old daughter of cofounder Pervis Spann, is owner of the station. Last year she entered into an unprecedented agreement with Clear Channel, a partnership that she believes is key to her survival and growth.

Chauncey Bailey, the slain journalist from Oakland, California, was part of a black-owned cable venture called

OUR TV. Just three months before his untimely murder, I had the opportunity to speak with him and his partner, Leonard Stephens, about their dedication to community access television.

While there were only about thirty African American–owned radio and television stations in 1976, today there are about 260. Progress—albeit modest. And yet, most of this growth occurred during the 1970s and '80s. Not only have such gains come to a screeching halt since then, but the tide has, in fact, moved in the opposite direction.

It seems almost impossible to believe that people of color, who make up 33 percent of the national population, own just 3.6 percent of the fourteen hundred commercial broadcast television stations in America. Women, of all races, own just 5 percent of such stations. Broadcast television ownership among minority women has not been officially calculated, to my knowledge, by any government or nonprofit agency.

The most accurate numbers that do exist come from groundbreaking research released by the Free Press, a Washington, DC, media reform group. The organization took on the work of compiling the study in 2006 because the federal government stopped collecting data on minority ownership in 2000 and has refused to do so ever since. With such embarrassingly low numbers, and no plans in place to improve minority ownership, it is no wonder. New data would only invite increased scrutiny and criticism of misguided FCC policies.

According to the Free Press report, the largest African American–owned broadcaster is the New York–based

Granite Broadcasting, which filed for bankruptcy soon
after this report was released in December of 2006. If
Granite loses its status as a black-owned company due to
restructuring, total black ownership of television stations
in the United States will fall, from about 1 percent to 0.64
percent.

In 1999, I published *Color by Fox: the Fox Network and
the Revolution in Black Television.* The book wasn't about
ownership, but at signings and press appearances I was
repeatedly asked, "Why don't we own anything? Why
don't we have any other television networks besides BET?"
Sold to Viacom in 2001, BET is no longer black owned.

I decided to write this book because I wanted readers to
meet some of the few remaining black owners of television
and radio. Most of them operate quietly and with very different agendas from the more widely publicized example
of BET. In many cases, they have had a profound impact
on their local communities. I wanted readers to know that
far too many black- and woman-owned stations have been
sold over the past three decades. The trend is not good.
Even now, many black-owned stations are passing into the
hands of large, mostly white-owned conglomerates and
monopoly owners.

Finally, informed consumers need to understand that
unlike policy makers of the 1970s, today's FCC does not
place any importance whatsoever on minority media ownership. For the past decade or so, it has actually encouraged
big owners to get bigger, while allowing smaller, minority
owners to be squeezed out of the industry entirely.

Why does this matter?

It matters because black women were the single seg-
ment of the U.S. population most adamantly opposed to a
war in Iraq, right from the start. Only 33 percent supported President George W. Bush's decision to go to war,
as opposed 70 percent of Americans in general. It matters
because African Americans, just 13 percent of the population, make up as much as 30 percent of all army personnel
currently serving in Iraq.

Ownership matters because while 93 percent of African
Americans disapproved of Bush's handling of the situation after Hurricane Katrina in 2005, only 66 percent of
white Americans felt the same way. The majority of black
people also believed that the government's response would
have been faster had victims been predominantly white.
As Bob Bullard, director of the Environmental Justice
Resource Center at Clark Atlanta University, has said,
black people were simply "the wrong complexion for protection." Only 17 percent of white Americans agreed with
this assessment.

Media ownership matters, I tell my journalism students
at Hofstra University, because the perceptions and life
experiences of people of color are often wildly divergent
from those of the general population. As one writer noted,
white people are always horrified and gasp aloud when she
confesses to them that her grandfather was a Klansman.
Black people, she says, don't even bat an eye.

Media ownership matters because black women are four
times more likely to have Type II diabetes than white
women, and because African Americans are eight times

more likely to be diagnosed with HIV than non-blacks. African American are also five times more likely to die of asthma and twenty-three times more likely to die of cancer.

These differences in perception and experience matter when we, as members of the media, decide how to tell a story.

In the days and weeks following Hurricane Katrina, the mainstream media often showed one photo that soon became famous. It was the image of an anonymous dead body slumped in a wheelchair—abandoned and covered with a plaid-patterned blanket. We saw the image, and yet almost no major media outlets bothered to tell the story of that anonymous woman. I went to New Orleans to learn more about ninety-one-year-old Ethel Freeman, a retired custodian who used a feeding tube and was forced to wear diapers due to illness. Her son, Herbert Freeman, Jr., took her to the convention center by boat, where they waited four days for food, water, and medical care that never came. Mrs. Freeman died waiting. When her son was ordered by national guardsmen with guns to get on a bus, he wrote his name and a cell phone number on a scrap of paper and pinned it to his dead mother's clothing.

Journalists have an eye for finding depth and emotion in everyday human stories. But what good does it do us if there are no outlets in which to publish our work?

Ownership matters. Study after study has shown that minority broadcast owners report more local news, have more diverse hiring and management, and serve their communities better.

African Americans are not alone in our perception that something is deeply wrong with today's news coverage. Of 12,600 news stories from 2005, the National Hispanic Media Coalition found that less than 1 percent were about Latinos, or featured issues important to Latinos. "We're basically invisible except when we're criminals," noted Ivan Roman, executive director of the National Association of Hispanic Journalists.

Because of the infamous 1996 Telecommunications Act, which relaxed ownership limits even further, the media giant Clear Channel went from being a company with thirty-six radio stations to one that now owns and operates more than twelve hundred stations. This means that in many cities, the same company controls as many as seven or eight major stations.

And yet, in 2003, the Republican-led FCC tried to relax ownership rules even further. The commission proposed that companies could have 45 percent of television audiences in major markets, instead of 35 percent. In addition, they could own a newspaper and a television station in the same city under these rules. The five major media conglomerates already own 70 percent of prime time broadcast television markets, in addition to most cable, and much of radio, publishing, movie studios, music, Internet, and other related sectors. But that is not enough. Five companies—Viacom, Disney, Time Warner, News Corp., and NBC/GE—maintain that further consolidation makes them more effective and better able to offer news.

By vast majority, the public disagrees.

Nearly three million complaints were sent to the FCC in opposition to its secret plans, which were crafted behind closed doors and did not allow for public comment. "It was a consumer victory," said Democratic Commissioner Michael Copps.

At FCC public hearings attended by Copps and the only other Democratic commissioner currently in office, Jonathan Adelstein, thousands of ordinary citizens waited in line for hours, sometimes in sleeping bags and tents, as they did in San Antonio, Texas, to express their discontent with these plans.

At one such meeting in Los Angeles, I spoke with retired U.S. Army Lt. Col. Solomon Jamerson, a dignified, white-haired African American man who attended the hearing because he was opposed to media consolidation. When asked why, he said simply: "The first step to taking over a country is to take over its media." Citizens from all walks of life expressed outrage, bewilderment, and frustration at what they saw as a fundamental assault on democracy. And yet, almost no major media outlets covered these events.

Public frustration rose to the fore yet again in late 2006, when Senator Barbara Boxer (D-CA) exposed FCC deception and misuse of taxpayer dollars by revealing that two in-house reports from 2003 and 2004 had been destroyed in order to keep them from public view. One of the reports, compiled by the commission's own staff, showed that the number of radio station owners nationwide had fallen by 35 percent; proof that mass consolidation was taking place. The other revealed that local news was best covered by local news station owners, rather than by media conglomerates, as the FCC had originally claimed. They were "deep-sixed," as Boxer put it, because they presented evidence that went against the claims of the Republican-controlled commission.

The picture is grim. Although almost all small-station owners have been squeezed out of business, women and minorities have been hit hardest of all. But for all the public discontent, the Republican-controlled FCC remains undaunted. It still believes that monopoly policies are the way to go and that declining minority ownership is not a problem.

After appointing (under pressure) a twenty-nine-member Advisory Committee on Diversity in 2003, the volunteer members worked diligently for more than a year and a half to present eighteen specific recommendations for promoting minority and female broadcast ownership— one of which was to immediately reinstitute the Minority Tax Certificate.

But the FCC failed even to mention its recommendations in a 2006 notice of proposed rulemaking, says David Honig, executive director of the Minority Media and Telecommunications Council (MMTC) in Washington, DC, and one of the advisory panel members.

At the Los Angeles hearing in 2006, the only one attended by all five of the commissioners (also under pressure), I couldn't help but notice how profoundly ill at ease the FCC chair Kevin Martin appeared to be. Fidgeting in his chair, distracted, and strikingly young for his post at age forty, he apparently had no idea how to respond to the audience's whooping and heckling of the commission's failed policies. Again and again, ordinary citizens made the point: the airwaves are public resources. They belong to the people. As I watched Martin squirm, I wondered how it was that someone charged with protecting the public's interest could be so uncomfortable listening to the public.

CHAPTER 1

JAMES L. WINSTON

For nearly three decades, Jim Winston, sixty, has served as executive director of the National Association of Black-Owned Broadcasters (NABOB), which describes itself as "the first and largest trade organization representing the interests of African American owners of radio and television stations across the country." Founded in 1976 "by a small group of African American broadcasters," NABOB has been a staunch advocate for minority owners. A fundamental belief at the core of the organization, says Winston, is that African Americans can never hope to have real economic and political power without genuine access to the mass media.

In addition to holding annual conferences and other educational and networking opportunities, NABOB and its 258 members (245 radio and 13 television stations) have contested the means by which Arbitron, the nation's premier radio audience researcher, is using new technologies to measure listeners. The company's new Portable People Meter significantly undercounts African American listeners, according to Winston and other NABOB members, resulting in a significant decline in advertising dollars for black owners.

But there is more to Jim Winston's story than his laudable work with NABOB. After serving as a legal assistant at the FCC from 1978 to 1980, he was also an aspiring owner of television. Winston's long-ago foray into the world of media ownership is a memory that perhaps he himself might prefer to forget, but it reveals some of the almost insurmountable challenges that would-be black owners have faced when trying to establish a foothold in broadcasting and cable media ownership.

*   *   *

Let's start at the beginning. How did the Minority Ownership Policy come about?

The shaping of it began in 1974, in a case called the TV 9 case, where the District of Columbia U.S. Court of Appeals told the FCC that it could not ignore the effects of past racial discrimination in choosing applicants for broadcast licenses. As a result, the FCC added race to its criteria in considering potential owners. At the time, if more than one party applied for a new broadcast license, the FCC would decide who to give it to by holding formal "comparative hearings" in which the various applicants were considered. It already had what it called "enhancement credits" if, for example, the applicant was local to the community or planned to work full time at the station. These all worked in their favor. With the Minority Policy

Statement, they added race as a factor in that list of considerations.

So this was a big step?

Yes. Shortly thereafter, the FCC at the urging of Commissioner Benjamin Hooks, who was the first African American Commissioner, began a rulemaking proceeding to determine what other policies the FCC might adopt to promote minority ownership.

In addition to minority enhancements, they adopted two other policies.

One was the distress sale policy.

Yes. That said that if a broadcast station licensee was in jeopardy of losing their license due to rule violations, the FCC would allow them to sell to a minority company for no more than 75 percent of fair market value. Previously if you were being investigated for serious rule violations, you were not allowed to sell the station until the investigation was over, and some cases would be litigated for years. So this allowed some bad actors to get out of the industry, and allowed some new minority owners to get in.

The tax certificate policy was also part of the Minority Policy Statement.

Right, which worked as follows: If I am the owner of a station and I choose to sell it, I have to pay IRS capital gains taxes, which at the time was 20 percent. This means that if I make $6 million, I will owe $1.2 million in taxes.

With the minority tax certificate policy, if I sell to a minority, I can defer capital gains tax for two years.

So this was a major shift.

Major. It felt like a big change was coming. And a big change did come.

In what sense?

In 1978, there was only one African American–owned television station and about forty African American–owned radio stations. Just two years later, there were ten African American–owned TV stations and 140 African American–owned radio stations.

Then what happened?

In 1981, Ronald Reagan took office. He appointed Mark Fowler chairman of the FCC, who was the first ever to oppose the tax certificate and the Minority Ownership Policy. Before that, both Democrats and Republicans supported it. For the first several years, Mark Fowler's attacks had no major impact. He would try to hold things up at the commission, but the votes were usually there to support the policy. It was a gradual attack. After that meteoric rise in minority ownership, there was still some growth, but it was much slower from 1981 through 1995.

What happened in 1995?

That's when the ax fell. In January, two things went wrong: Republicans took control of the House and Senate, and a minority entrepreneur [see Frank Washington interview] announced that he was buying cable systems for $2.3 billion. The problem was that the money was all being put up by TCI [former cable operator Tele-Communications, Inc., now known as Liberty Media]. So the first thing the Republicans saw was that there was going to be this tax certificate issued to what appeared to be a minority fronting for TCI. So they said this program is an outrage and needs to be abolished. They said it encouraged shams.

But was the program flawed?

We pointed out from 1978 through 1995 there had been hundreds of tax certificates and very few of them had ever even been questioned. And that they were certainly nothing even remotely like the transaction in front of them. We also argued that the FCC had the authority to deny a tax certificate for any transaction. All they had to do was to investigate it and see whether or not it was legitimate. They didn't have to abolish the whole program because of one bad deal.

But that one bad deal came at the perfect political moment.

That's all they needed. So they swept it right out of Congress. I know that Frank Washington was at the FCC when the Minority Policy was adopted in 1978, so I think he had some regard for the program. But not enough regard for the program, as it turned out, because he should never have done that transaction. It was a very bad transaction at the worst possible moment.

Clinton was in office at the time.
Right, he signed the Telecommunications Act of 1996.

But it was slipped into a bill that gave small business owners a deduction on health insurance.
Right, they slipped that in on him. So he's got a lot to regret. He's my favorite president, but he didn't get it all right.

Let's go back to those early days when everyone was feeling optimistic. As a matter of fact, I know that you and two other former FCC attorneys, Booker Wade and Sam Cooper, got together and tried to buy a television station, Community Television Network.
Wow, you're like the CIA. You're getting deep into it. I haven't heard that mentioned in many years.

I don't think it's been discussed lately.
Well, we never got off the ground, that's why.

Why not?
Well, we were sitting there in 1980 trying to get our business off the ground when Jimmy Carter lost the election. All our friends at the FCC who would have helped us get started got swept out of office, and Mark Fowler and his constituency came in. They decided they would create a bunch of rules for television that made it virtually impossible for stations like ours to ever get off the ground.

But you had quite a lot of funding. Gene Autry [a radio, television and film star known as "the singing cowboy" in the 1940s and '50s] helped to finance the venture.
That's right.

It seemed like it was ready to go.
Okay, here's what happened. There was no such thing as a low-power television service at the time. Instead, the FCC licensed television translators, which would then rebroadcast the signal of a main station. So we asked for a waiver of the television translator rule. We said, "Let us use these low-power transmitters as if they were regular television stations." Historically, the FCC has allowed people to come in with new ideas for new services and given them waivers so that they could get off the ground, and we think that the previous commission would have granted it as a matter of discretion. Instead, Fowler's FCC put our request on hold. Then they had a rulemaking proceeding that went on for years to develop rules for low-power television service. Instead of letting us get started while they developed a policy, they stopped us. Later, the Gene Autry money was no longer available, and the industry had changed such that our business plan no longer worked for low-power television. Plus, they put low-power stations into lotteries so that you couldn't be sure that you would get the licenses you were trying to get.

Why do you think they took this position against you?

Fowler was on record as being opposed to affirmative action. So I think you can assume that that was part of his overall philosophy.

What did you do next?

I decided to open my own law firm [Rubin, Winston, Diercks, Harris & Cooke in Washington, DC], and NABOB needed an executive director. Since they had limited financial resources, we made an arrangement where I would run it out of my law office.

Did you take yourself out of the ownership game completely?

Yeah, I think so. That was a rough time. We personally lost money, all three of us, as a result of that. So that was my one foray into ownership. I needed to concentrate on making a steady income after that.

Did you lose your shirt?

I lost my shirt. But I'm still here. I'm clothed again.

Can you talk a little bit about the history of NABOB?

NABOB was founded in the mid–1970s by a small group of black owners like Percy Sutton of Inner City Broadcasting. A few of the families are still in the business, like "Skip" Carter, whose family was one of the first to purchase a radio station, in 1950. It's still owned by his grandson, Michael Carter, KPRS in Kansas City. And Andrew Langston, who is still running his station up in

Rochester, New York, WVKX. . . . Each of the early founders was separately a pioneer in their own right, and most of them did not even know that there were other black broadcast stations around the country. They were brought together at a National Association of Broadcasters (NAB) conference, and when they got acquainted they realized they all had similar problems, such as advertisers not appreciating the value of the African American consumer. So they decided to join together to educate advertisers. That was one goal. The second was to increase the number of African American owners. These are the same objectives that we have now, thirty years later.

What can you tell us about Percy Sutton, who is the cofounder, together with his son Pierre, of Inner City Broadcasting?

Percy is like the beginning. You know, it was 1972, and they were the first ones to get a big successful station. For a long time, WBLS was the number-one station in New York.

How was he able to be so successful?

Percy Sutton was a successful attorney, and he was also the first African American to be borough president of Manhattan, so that gave him a lot of contacts. He's one of the most charismatic people you'll ever meet: a very smart, very shrewd businessman. And he parlayed that into a number of business ventures that led to his owning the radio stations.

You must feel very strongly about this issue to have stayed with the organization for all these decades.

Yes, yes, decades. Indeed. And obviously, I feel very sad about the way it's gone. We've had some companies that have been successful but the total number of owners continues to decline. Seeing the industry consolidate is disappointing. It's a sad state, and it seems to be getting worse every day. Certainly, African Americans have done well in comparison to where we were one hundred years ago, but in comparison to the American pie and how it's divided, our slice is still miniscule.

I wanted to talk a little bit about one of the "little guys" who is currently being squeezed out by big owners. You now represent your former business partner, Booker Wade, in his lawsuit against AT&T. What that's about?

Booker is now general manager of a noncommercial television station in San Francisco, KMTP, which I have been representing for maybe six or seven years. This started actually even before AT&T took over the cable system there. I think it was Comcast that bought a bunch of cable systems in the San Francisco area in 2000 and advised Booker they were dropping KMTP. They just looked up one day, and they weren't being carried.

Why don't the cable companies want to carry KMTP?

Well, because they can make much more money if they put on A&E or HGTV or some other cable channel instead.

Booker says their strategy is "to choke us to death so that we die."
Yeah. That's the strategy.

Do you think it's more about greed than race?
It's America. Can you say it's only one of those things, or that the other has no bearing whatsoever? If you've grown up black in America, it's hard to believe that race is never a factor.

I mean the irony is that Comcast later partnered with TV One [the African American–oriented cable network founded with Radio One in 2004] to make more money.
Yes, yes. Thank you. It's America. The best business people see only green.

How is the KMTP battle related to the larger issue of minority ownership?
Well, they're noncommercial, so Booker Wade is not an owner. The station is run by a community board. But in terms of getting access to diverse programming, it's similar.

Where is the case now?
It's been pending at the commission since 2000. We had a preliminary decision that went against us on two different counts, and now we've got an appeal pending.

You have to admire Booker Wade. He hung with it all these years.
Booker's the most tenacious person I've ever met.

Do you think people would be upset about the KMTP lawsuit if they knew about it?

It's a pretty narrow issue. If you don't watch the station in San Francisco, you'd never even know there was an issue. And the people who can't see us on the cable system that we've never been on don't even know that they miss us.

Would they be upset if they knew?

I think if you told them BET was being kept off the cable system or TV One was being kept off the cable system, they'd be outraged. If you told them it was noncommercial programming, my guess is they would say, "Well, we don't watch that much noncommercial programming."

Are you a little bit cynical?

You beat your head against the wall long enough, you know, it does affect your outlook. I try to be optimistic. . . . What I know is that we had good policies in place that worked very well. We started at less than 1 percent and got as high as about 2 percent with the minority ownership policies in place. But what caused them to stop working was a change in the political structure in Washington.

Do you ever speak to the general public about these issues—at colleges or community forums?

I go where I'm invited, mostly industry conferences and meetings. And every election cycle NABOB has done public service announcements on media consolidation, but unfortunately the general public misses most of this. It's going right past them.

Why don't more black owners come to you for help?

The sad part is that some owners come and go without ever touching base with NABOB. There's always someone struggling to start something, get something moving, and I often hear about it after they fail. We have conferences, we bring in speakers. It's interesting because the common answer I get is, "Well, I couldn't afford to come to Washington." But then later we find out that you couldn't afford *not* to come because you might have stayed in business if you had.

I talked to a former owner who has owned a couple of small radio stations, and when I asked him if the 1996 Telecom Act impacted him, he said he honestly didn't know.

It's really quite amazing. There are so many people who don't understand the fundamentals of being a business person. There are people who buy radio stations the same way they buy gas stations. People who can put together the money will give the seller $20,000, and the seller takes back a note for $80,000. What they don't know is that they bought a $100,000 radio station that's only worth $20,000. They don't even know what they did wrong. And when they finally call NABOB, it's after the fact.

It's too late.

A guy calls me two months ago. He's bought a $200,000 radio station and paid the buyer $165,000. The buyer has a note for $35,000. So he defaulted on the $35,000 note, and the buyer took the station back. He got it backwards. He's paid this guy $165,000 on a $200,000 purchase, but the guy never transferred the license to him, which is absurd. So the man wants to complain to the FCC. I said, "Sir, the FCC's records show that this man has been the owner of this station nonstop. You don't show up in any of their records. There's nothing for them to protect. You don't own anything."

This is a true story?

This happened two months ago.

Wow. Was this his first loan?

First everything, I guess. You know, you asked me before if I was a little jaded. I went home and told my wife this story, and she said, "Oh, this is terrible. Do something for him." I said, "There's nothing I can do for him. I've just heard too many of these stories." And I asked the guy, "Why did you sign an agreement like this without a lawyer?" He said he had a local lawyer. You know, you go home and dream about this and just wake up in the morning upset. Because you know you can't help him. It's a very sad story. Well, he sounded like a young man. He'll recover. He'll get a new shirt.

CHAPTER 2

CATHERINE LIGGINS HUGHES

When Cathy Hughes, sixty, Radio One chairperson and founder, bought her first radio station in 1980 in Washington, DC, many listeners, investors, and advertisers disapproved of her all-talk format, saying that news programming would never turn a profit. She became host of her own informational talk show, as she raised her son Alfred, born when she was just seventeen. Many of her local callers were struggling, single mothers just like her. She was chastised by the black bourgeoisie, she says, who didn't appreciate her opening the phone lines to an audience that "chewed up its verb tenses" and embarrassed the Washington elite.

Before winning approval on a loan from a Latina rookie at Chemical Bank, Hughes says that she had the doors of thirty-two financial institutions slammed in her face by men. And this, despite the fact that she was the first woman station manager in the city—at Howard University's WHUR—and that she increased annual billing there from $250,000 to $3 million in little more than a year.

The story of Radio One, the largest urban radio network in the country, and Hughes's tenacious rise to fame, is well-known in industry circles. She once walked into a meeting with a potential investor, her trademark blonde bob neatly coifed, not knowing that she needed a business plan. When asked for such a document, she was momentarily perplexed. "My plan is to succeed in business," she responded matter-of-factly.

When Hughes ran out of money, she made the radio station (a former drug den) her temporary home, cooking on a hotplate. She persevered. For her, radio was "the talking drum" of the community, and she kept it alive with missionary zeal.

In 1999, Hughes became "officially rich," as her son, Alfred Liggins, thirty-nine—Radio One president and CEO and now TV One chairman—has said. Liggins had gone off to earn an MBA from Wharton College, and returned home with big ideas for the company. It was at his urging that Hughes took Radio One public, becoming the first African American woman to do so. Heading to Wall Street was not easy for Hughes, who still describes herself as "a black nationalist." She worried about losing control, about falling out of touch with her community. But in the end she had to make a decision, and "it was either grow or die." The company is now valued at more than $3 billion.

TV One, a joint venture between Radio One, which is now the nation's largest black-oriented radio broadcaster, and Comcast, the nation's largest cable company, launched on the Martin Luther King, Jr. holiday, January 18, 2004, in more than two million households. Today, it is seen in forty million homes. And still, Cathy Hughes remains nostalgic about her roots in radio. "I love radio," she says. "I breathe it. I live it. I feel so blessed that I have a career in it. I would have worked at a radio station whether they paid me or not."

*   *   *

For a black woman to own a radio station was rare at the end of the 1970s. How did you come to buy your first station, talk radio WOL-AM 1450?

While working at WHUR at Howard University, I created a program called *The Quiet Storm*, which in the short period of eighteen months became the number-one show in Washington. It went on to become the most popular format in the history of urban radio. In its heyday, it was on more than five hundred stations. Even today, there are several radio stations that call themselves "The Quiet Storm." But Howard University punished me for creating the format because I replaced their avant-garde jazz program.

Why was that a problem?

Well, the jazz enthusiasts raised hell, so the university was very punitive with me.

Punitive how?

They docked my pay for three weeks while I was on jury duty. They would write me up constantly . . . they cut my budget. I didn't have money to pay the host, and I ended up paying him personally, out of my own paycheck. It was just a litany of punitive actions they took to try to get me to abandon the format.

At Howard you were the first woman radio station general manager in the city of Washington, DC. Did gender play a role in the conflict?

I think so. My direct report was a retired military general who had been in Vietnam. He said that he didn't think women were emotionally suited to run radio stations.

So how did you decide that ownership was the way to go?

Because of *The Quiet Storm*, Smokey Robinson's career was resurrected, and he was willing to sign over the publishing rights to his song. I wanted Howard to copyright the format and get a trademark so that they could license it. We were on more than five hundred stations, and they literally could have been generating tens of millions of dollars each year, but they refused to do it.

Why?

Because it was controversial. The jazz enthusiasts were literally picketing outside the station. They were fighting me tooth and nail to take it off.

Did they think that it watered down black culture?

That's what they said. They called it bubble gum. Because again we're talking about [people] who are part of the intelligentsia; they look down their noses at R&B.

So how did this conflict lead you to believe you should own a radio station?

Well, when I tried to convince Howard to copyright the format, and they wouldn't, I saw that they just literally blew, by now, probably $100 million. Just let it slip through their hands, alright? So I made up my mind then that the next time God blessed me with an original idea, I would be in total control of it. I would not be going through anyone else. That's why I wanted to go into business, so that I could control my own professional destiny.

How were you able to buy WOL?

The FCC had recently passed the distress sale policy, which meant that if your station was in trouble, and if you discounted the price by a third and sold it either to a woman or a person of color, you wouldn't have to lose it completely. WOL in Washington was the first distress sale after the policy was passed.

Why did you choose an all-talk format? That was also controversial wasn't it?

[Laughs] Everyone loves to call me controversial. I prefer to use the word provocative. Well, we did what is called a "format search" to research the market and identify what listeners believe is missing. The results came back that they wanted to hear "news talk from a black perspective."

At the time, Washington, DC, was 72 percent African American. Are you familiar with the term "Talented Tenth?"

Absolutely.

Well, in Washington they wanted a voice, and they wanted the ability to express themselves. Howard University is a hub of black intelligentsia. But you've also got Catholic University, Georgetown, American University. People forget that Washington, DC, is not only the capital, it's also a college town. You've got Federal City College, which is now the University of the District of Columbia, and Notre Dame in Baltimore. So you're talking about a large percentage of individuals on the faculty and staff and among the student body who are African American.

But the station wasn't just for the so-called Talented Tenth. You had listeners from all walks of life and economic levels calling in. In fact, some of the black elites disapproved of the callers you chose to put on the air.

Oh, I can't tell you how much of a battle that was. I had school teachers who actually wrote petitions saying that I was setting the race back. They thought those who may not have been as articulate or as proficient with the King's English were embarrassing the race. But you have to understand, this is a community where even the crack addicts read *The Washington Post*. People are well-informed here. You don't have the level of misinformation that you would have in other metropolitan areas. Some individuals who may have been high school dropouts, or who may put an extra "s" on a word, were in fact totally knowledgeable about what was going on in a war zone, or with the economy. They may not have used the correct English to express themselves but they knew what they were talking about.

You have said that radio is the talking drum of the community.
Information really is power. The older I get the more adamant I become about this. I saw radio as the heir to black newspapers and we all know the role that black newspapers played in the liberation of African Americans. Black folks will make the right decisions when they are given the right information in a timely manner. Our biggest problem, though, is that we normally get information when it becomes history, so we are always in this reactionary posture. My desire for WOL was to allow all walks of black life to express themselves and to talk to each other. It kind of started a revolution because now we have a Tom Joyner morning show, which is syndicated in 120 cities. Steve Harvey now has a syndicated morning show. All of these are a direct result of WOL being the first to say black folks want to know about more than just the latest Michael Jackson record.

You have said that one of your greatest inspirations was Katherine Graham, former owner and publisher of The Washington Post.

Yes, she was my She-ro. After Watergate, I was inspired and committed to bringing that level of service to my community. And it wasn't easy for her either. She was sued and ostracized. She went through hell and high water.

Do you think with the sharp decline in African American ownership of radio that we're at risk of losing the talking drum?

Absolutely. While the sign of the times is syndication, it scares me because for Tom Joyner to be in 120 markets, that means that 119 other morning show hosts don't have jobs. That's real. But I think what is so strong about Tom Joyner is that he's more active in keeping historically black colleges alive than the United Negro College Fund.

Yes.

Every single, solitary day Tom is beating the drum about historically black colleges, whereas UNCF only gets the opportunity to do it once a year. Okay? And it really is about changing people's minds. It's not just about making them aware. I'm certain UNCF would love to have the opportunity to reach so many people, but for Tom to be able to constantly give out the scholarships, and raise the money, and talk about the schools . . . history will probably write that Tom Joyner saved black colleges.

In 2005, you launched TV One. I know that the cable channel is mostly your son Alfred's baby, but can you talk about why it hs been so hard for African Americans to launch cable networks?

I think most of the heads of broadcasting networks came up through the civil rights era, and they at least had an awareness of the struggle. Cable, on the other hand, is run by younger men who weren't exposed to these ideas.

So you see the problem as being generational.

Let me give you a classic example. For years, Bob Johnson took heat from black people about what BET was not. But he never lied to anybody. He called it Black Entertainment Television and his target demo was twelve to twenty-four. Those kids weren't interested in listening to Tavis Smiley. They weren't interested in hearing news. They were interested in music videos, and that's what he gave them. That's the reason it turned out to be a $3 billion venture. But Bob would have loved to have other cable channels. He would have loved to have had a TV One under the BET umbrella. Discovery has several channels. They have Discovery Healthy, Discovery Life, Discovery Financial. There are many viable Latino channels. But all black folks ever had was BET because the industry would not allow anyone else to get their foot in the door, and it would not allow Bob to expand. And all of us, including myself, beat up on Bob so badly because we wanted BET to be everything to everybody.

I know that BET once considered launching a Black Family Channel, for example, but backed off of that idea fairly quickly. The Black Family Channel that did eventually come into

*existence, founded by civil rights attorney Willie Gary and for-
mer world champion boxer Evander Holyfield, was just sold.*
Gone. Okay? Because they couldn't get distribution.

And why is that?
Because he who controls distribution, controls the
wealth. It doesn't matter what arena you're in. That's the
reason you don't have independent black grocery stores.
That's why you don't have a daily black newspaper. That's
why *Essence* magazine is no longer black owned.

*So how were you able to launch TV-One and succeed where
others have failed?*
In cable, we have engaged in strategic alliances and rela-
tionships. That was the only way we could get our foot in
the door. With TV One, our partner is Comcast.

*Right, so it is only partially black owned. Going back to the
talking drum concept, what is the vision for TV One in terms
of offering news and information to the community?*
News doesn't exist there, as of yet, except in a very limited fashion. We have a public affairs program that is produced by Black Enterprise and that deals with financial
information. And we have America's Black Forum. But
right now, most of our news and information comes from
acquired programming because we're not in critical mass
yet, which for us is about sixty-five million. We are the
fastest-growing cable network—except when the NFL
locks in all the fellas for the football games. But the reality

is that until you get to a certain number in terms of viewers, you don't put a lot of money into original programming because no one's watching, and it's very costly.

What future plans do you have for news?

Ultimately, we will have a news service not only for TV One but that will also service Radio One, and we'll be able to sell that product as we do now. For instance, did you know that Melody's format [Melody Spann-Cooper of WVON in Chicago] is actually ours? The Al Sharpton show is actually a Radio One product that we sell to Melody. She has two shows that are hers, but the rest of the programming is acquired from us. So that's how we will do our news also.

I have often been a guest on your show Access One, *which has offered interviews with Barack Obama and major political figures. How do you see this program serving the community?*

All those talking heads programs are basically public affairs, but ultimately we want to have actual news. Jonathan [Rodgers, president of TV One] is a news man. He comes out of the discipline. Shows like *Access One* are our stop-gap programs until we get to critical mass and are able to really put money into a full-fledged news operation.

That sounds great.

And we not only want news, we want to be interactive also. I can't wait to do polls. I want to know what black folks have to say about questions like "Who really speaks for black America?" and "What does black America really want?" I can't wait to get that launched so that we can really say four thousand black folks voiced their opinion, logged in on this issue, and this is what they felt.

So you're looking forward to doing original reporting and original journalism.

Absolutely, my mission has always been information from a black perspective and news from a black perspective. I would like the opportunity to prove conventional wisdom wrong and to show that black folks will be just as receptive to hearing good things going on in the community as they have been to who got run over, hit by a car, arrested for crack-cocaine or murdered last night.

I've talked to some high-ranking staff members at TV One who do not feel the need to speak to overtly racial and political issues.

Well, I don't think they'd be brave enough to express that opinion to me. Community news to me is what we're all about. We're about giving a voice to the black community.

In our earlier conversations, when you were first launching, you said that even Alfred, and others of his generation who didn't have police dogs biting at them, don't necessarily see the need for the same kinds of programming as you do.

Yes, we still have that philosophical difference and that will always exist, but it doesn't have anything to do with what the mission of the company is about. I think the main difference is that he and I see the cable industry differently.

In what way?

He has a more optimistic view or a more "general market view," for want of a better description.

Getting back to the question of ownership, there was a time when you, too, were worried about changing FCC policies and how they might affect black ownership. But it seems that Alfred made those changing rules work for Radio One to the company's advantage. In 1993, he purchased WERQ-AM/FM in Baltimore for $9 million, forming the first black-owned duopoly in the nation.

Yes, absolutely. A triopoly, actually. Listen, I tried to spread the word. I went to conferences telling black folks that things are going to change, that consolidation is going to change the entire landscape. I was trying to sound the horn of alarm. And when these policies and rules became the reality, we either had to grow along with them or die. We had to adapt to the landscape.

And you did that fairly early on.

Absolutely. In the same way that Inner City Broadcasting has done. The fact that WBLS in New York is able to stay alive and continue to prosper is just remarkable, considering the fact that they're a stand alone that's competing against corporations that have five, six, seven stations in the market.

They've taken some heat recently for abandoning the black talk format at WLIB.

AM is a whole different animal. We just did a survey that blew us away. It was for young people, ages twelve to twenty-eight. Eighty-five percent of them had never heard of AM radio stations. They grew up with FM.

Where is your company looking in terms of future investments?

We're looking at print. We just acquired *Giant* magazine in December of 2006, and right now we're doing that with a big Internet initiative. Our goal is to have a multidimensional platform to reach the African American consumer.

Overall, what would you say about the lack of black ownership of radio and television?

At one time, radio was controlled by small family corporations. The wife of Lyndon Baines Johnson . . . Lady Bird was in the radio business. They were media folks. Families owned radio stations that are now owned by major corporations. And that's why we went public. We weren't big enough to survive alone. We knew we needed a whole lot more stations real quick to stay alive. Consolidation has done this.

Do you have any regrets about going public?

Yes and no. It was the right decision at the time.

CHAPTER 3

PERCY AND PIERRE SUTTON

One of the members of the so-called Gang of Four, attorney Percy Sutton, now eighty-seven, who served as Manhattan Borough president from 1966–1977, was part of a group of Harlem power brokers who dominated New York City politics from the 1950s through the 1970s. The group's members included Charlie Rangel, a member of the U.S. Congress from 1971 to the present; David Dinkins, a former member of the state legislature who became the city's first African American mayor in 1990; and Basil Paterson, a former state senator during the 1960s who was appointed New York's first African American secretary of state in 1979. All influential Harlem businessmen and public servants, the friends worked together as partners to recruit other powerful educators, clergy members, and entertainers to help launch a media company that would further the growth of black power in Harlem.

Their group venture was called Inner City Broadcasting, founded in 1972 by Percy Sutton and his son Pierre, then thirty-six years old, with the help of fifty-eight African American investors. Once the largest black-owned group

of radio stations in the country (a title now held by Radio
One), Inner City made its first foray into ownership with
the purchase of two New York radio stations, WLIB-AM
and WBLS-FM, whose guests included Percy Sutton's
most famous client, the revolutionary civil rights leader
Malcolm X, along with prominent members of the Black
Panther Party.

For decades, the stations have been known as a resource
for the people of Harlem and for African American community-based informational programming and music.
Recently, however, Inner City has been poised for change.

In 2001, WLIB's all-talk format was dropped and
replaced with Caribbean music. In 2004, CEO Pierre Sutton, now sixty, allowed the left-leaning, progressive network Air America to begin leasing time from the New
York station. As Percy Sutton explained to the press at the
time, defending his son's decision, "For thirty years, WLIB
has been geared to the black community, and not one year
have we been able to make it break even." If not for the
undisputed financial success of the company's sister station, WBLS, Inner City might never have stayed alive as
long as it has. In 2006, WLIB again switched to a gospel
"Praise and Inspiration" format—a change that was hotly
contested by community members who yearned for a
return to political talk about the issues of the day. Most
recently, the station has attempted to find a balance
between talk and music. Whatever the future direction of
Inner City, which sold its only television holdings—Urban
Cable of Philadelphia—to Time Warner in 2005, the

monumental historical importance of the Suttons, and their more than thirty years in broadcast ownership, is undeniable.

*   *   *

PERCY SUTTON

Let's begin by talking a bit about your family background. What did your parents do for a living?

My father was the colored superintendent of schools in San Antonio, Texas. You hear what I said, the "colored" superintendent.

Yes.

It's an awful thing that he had to be in a separate school. My mother was my first grade teacher, and six of my brothers and sisters were my teachers before I graduated from high school. I learned from my oldest brother, who was a Communist. He went to Russia and married a Russian Jewish woman.

You are known for being a member of the influential "Gang of Four." Can you talk about the beginnings of your political power in New York City?

I lost for eleven consecutive years in Harlem before I could win anything.

Yes, the first seat you won was in 1964 when you became a New York state assemblyman. In 1967, you became one of the first African American borough presidents.

I did a lot of revolutionary things in Manhattan. I started community boards. We called them district boards at the time. We had fun. The Gang of Four tried to help other people get power.

As a civil rights attorney and activist, what were some of the issues you were involved in?

I have a history of being in jail a number of times.

How many times have you been arrested?

Thirty-two times. I was in the most vicious penitentiary in America, Parchment Penitentiary in Mississippi. One of the most fascinating ones was, for me, in Washington, DC. Before the new highways, there was a Route 40. I headed the NAACP in New York at that time, and I gathered a group of people to protest a diner. I remember leading my people in and being told by a man more swarthy than me, "Nigger, you can't eat here." I said, "I will eat here." He said, "No, nigger. You'll get arrested." The man had me arrested, and we went to trial. I testified about what it was like to be hungry and not to be able to eat. [Pause] A nice white jury took twelve minutes to convict me [laughs hard]!

Wow.

But I had television cameras with me, and I learned how to use the media, white media.

What are you most proud of in your work for civil rights?

Coming out of Parchment Penitentiary in 1961 . . .
I started my Freedom Rides in Atlanta, Georgia. I really
wanted to get arrested in Atlanta because the jails were
better there [laughs]. So we got on this bus. And about
sixty miles outside of Atlanta, a number of cars came with
people with baseball bats, and they started hitting on our
bus . . . I learned to fly when I was very young, and I never
wanted the plane to go in the water and drown.

You served in World War II.

And in the Korean conflict. And I remembered that and
that if they burned the bus, I would die like I didn't want
to die. And the veins in my head began to swell, and I
massaged them. We finally made it into the lunch counter.
We were on the way to Montgomery, Alabama, which is
where I had been at the military law school. I was selected
to become a lawyer because there were no black lawyers at
that time in the military.

I see.

And I remember seeing a young, black man—a
shoeshine man killed on the steps of the state capitol.
These things stayed with me. So when we got to the lunch
counter, we were about to go down the steps, and a man
stepped in front of us and flashed his FBI license and said,
"I'm here to help you. Please go swiftly to the counter and
move out because there's a very dangerous crowd here." He
walked in front of us, and we sat at the counter. And
I remember the lady at the counter said, "What do you

want nigger?" And I remember responding [high-pitched voice] "Orange juice, please!"

You were scared.

I was scared to death. People were screaming . . . and she slid it down the counter. We got out of there quickly and stayed in a safe house that night. A young man by the name of Martin Luther King, Jr., was a pastor there, and he arranged a safe house for us.

In 1964, you began putting together resources and talking to investors about buying what would become the first black-owned radio station in New York. Why was media ownership important?

When I was a kid in San Antonio, Texas, they wouldn't even let me in the door of the radio station! I was a civil rights activist. I wanted to talk about discrimination, and when I got to the door, they blocked me. I swore then that one day I would own that station, and eventually I did. It didn't make anybody rich! But I owned it.

How did you come to buy WLIB-AM, the first black-owned station in New York City?

At the time, I was representing Malcolm X, the revolutionary. And I represented some members of the Communist party. And by being an activist and going to jail with regularity in the civil rights struggle, I spoke out and defended revolutionaries and was able to attract people in the early days because of who I was. So I was able to gain access to a variety of opportunities, to make money and to lose money. I lost a lot of money when I was here [at Inner City]. And I lost money in the Apollo Theater, my own money and Inner City's money. Almost $30 million.

Yes.

Then I took Inner City with me to Africa and lost some more money, along with my own.

What were you trying to do in Africa?

Only 3 percent of all the people in African countries have access to a telephone. I wanted to install satellite. So because I was chairman of Inner City, and people voted with me, I said let's go to Africa. And we went there and lost money [laughs].

After Inner City bought WLIB, it switched from all music to a more politicized talk format.

Well, we were political but not stupid. Occasionally, comments would be made by members of the Communist party and occasionally comments would be made by Malcolm X. . . . But you can't let some of the people who want to be heard come onto the air. You have to balance it so that you can stay alive. We were not about to drive ourselves out of business. We were careful. If we allowed every voice on, nobody would advertise with us.

What memories do you have of Malcolm X?

After they tried to bomb his house in Queens, I was in court with him. And we left Queens to come to Manhattan, and we got in a car. . . . To my left was a man with a shotgun against the door and a pistol in his lap, and another man to my right, same thing. In the back was Minister Malcolm, and to his left was a man with a rifle or a shotgun and a pistol. And I remember turning around to the minister and asking, "Does this frighten you?" And he said, "No. I have a destiny." Within forty-one days he was slaughtered.

Wow. Shifting gears a bit, why do you think so many black-owned media ventures have failed?

Because of the absence of advertising. We have found, in every aspect, that advertising agencies will block you, especially blacks.

The National Association of Black-Owned Broadcasters, or NABOB, was founded to try to address this disparity.

My son was a part of that. I wasn't trying to build an organization. For me, it was a struggle to stay alive.

Looking back at your career as a lawyer, prominent civil rights activist, and media owner, what's most satisfying to you?

Having been in that jail with Stokely Carmichael and other revolutionaries. . . . If I had a choice of being black or white, I would have chosen being black because I like the way I grew up. I like the fact that my family was a family of protestors. I like the fact that some of them were Communists. I like all of that. And if you say Percy Sutton, most people, if they've had any involvement at all in protest in this society, they'll know me. And that's satisfying.

To know you played a role.
  That's right.

* * *

PIERRE SUTTON

What is the ownership structure of Inner City today?

It is still privately owned. Some of the original investors have passed on or delivered shares to their heirs. Most are still black, and there are some institutions.

Is it still in the control of the Sutton family?

Yes, we still control it. My father correctly sees himself as the chairman emeritus and as the trustee of the family. I was the incorporating president of Inner City Broadcasting in 1972. My father came into the company as chairman of the board in 1980 and left in 1990.

Was buying a radio station your idea or your father's?

I was operating a newspaper out of the basement of a brownstone in Harlem, the *New York Courier*, which I had from 1968 to 1972. In 1972, I sold it to the *Amsterdam News*. Before that I was in Vietnam. During the riots of 1968, my father was on the radio, on WLIB-AM, which was located in Harlem. He was borough president of Manhattan and when he spoke, I guess it had some positive effect. The owner, Harry Novick [who was white] spoke to him about buying the station. I guess the riots in Harlem and the civil unrest of the time kind of helped in that regard [laughs]. And he said that he would sell to my father.

Did you always know you wanted to go into media?

As a matter of fact, when I came back from Vietnam I got myself in a bit of trouble because I was opposed to the war, and I was writing about it. It created some conflict because I was still in the service. It wasn't a smart thing for me to do.

Kind of guerrilla journalism?

Yes, and that led to my going into the newspaper business. My father had always been interested in the power of the media because he was in public service. So when the time was right, and Novick decided to sell, my father decided to put together a group of his contemporaries to buy it. They included, for example, Judge "Cut 'Em Loose Bruce," who was famous in New York at the time. The *Daily News* called him "Cut Em Loose Bruce" because he would insist that black folks should get the same kind of treatment as white folks for the same crimes. Jesse Jackson was also involved as an investor.

And the famous Grammy award–winning musical artist Roberta Flack—

Roberta Flack. Also Dr. Roscoe Brown, who served with my father in the Tuskegee Airmen and was one of the first to shoot down a German jet with the propellers of an airplane. He serves on my board now, and I value his counsel.

The investors were all preachers and teachers and educators who saw the value in owning that little daytime radio station at the corner of 125th and Lenox Avenue. But if you can imagine, it took sixty-three people to put together a mere $246,000 for the down payment. The purchase price was $1.9 million. At the same time, we secured an option for the FM radio station, WLIB, for $1.1 million.

People thought AM was worth more back then.

Yes, it was worth more. FM signals would bounce off the leaves and the trees and the buildings, and you couldn't easily receive the signal. But this fellow up in Boston named Mitch Hastings developed something called the Circular Polarized Antennae, which enabled people to receive FM signals. I went up to Boston and talked to him. He had a metal plate in his head, and he knew radio. He was an engineer who owned an FM station up there, WBOS, and he had figured out how to make that FM station work. So we used that antenna and became number one in New York in 1977. We even outrated ABC, which had been number one for thirty years.

You probably never dreamed that FM would be the money-maker over your AM.

No, not initially. You know, it was fortuitous that we found out about the Circular Polarized Antennae before anyone else did. As luck would have it. But it wasn't just luck. Black music has always had an appeal across the board. But the thing about black radio is that it was unattractive to white folks in the way in which it was presented. You had shouting deejays talking jive, and commercials which were not highend. You know, they were selling prayer bricks and holy cloths in a basement for ten dollars down . . . stuff that really isn't appealing. So we took a high road. Our presenters, as we called them—not deejays—were all fairly well-educated and spoke knowledgeably about the music. The effect was that WLBS had a large, sophisticated appeal.

You had to have a lot of foresight to buy an FM station.

It wasn't foresight. It was fortunate because we secured the option for a nominal sum of money. The previous owner, Novick, didn't buy that station. All of the original licenses that the FCC let were granted for free. That was the early days of radio when they were giving the signals out to white people. Novick put black folks in buses and went down to the FCC and asked for the AM signal. And he was able to convince the commission that these poor people in Harlem needed to have an FM signal as well. He got both of them for nothing, and we got them for a nominal sum.

Of course, none of the stations were ever given away to African Americans in the early days of radio.

No.

Dorothy Brunson is also interviewed in this book. What was her role at Inner City in the early 1970s?

Dorothy Brunson is a good hustler. I brought her in as a general manager. She was a strong woman . . . and a tough customer.

Do you ever express your political views on your stations?

Occasionally, when I see a need. When apartheid was still in place, and they tried to sell the Krugerrand [the South African gold coin] in New York in the 1980s, we stopped that. I do editorials. I'm credited to some measure, at least by *The Village Voice*, for having done a lot to get Bloomberg elected as mayor. He's a Republican; I'm a Democrat. But the Democrats were wrong, and he was right.

Where do you see WLIB going in the future?

Well, context is everything. We never made any money on WLIB. Up to this point, the only three things you've been able to do on AM radio have been news, talk, and sports. . . . Let me put it to you like this: Malcolm X was my godfather. My father was his lawyer. Malcolm X was in my house all the time when I was a kid. He was perceived to have said, "Arm yourself. Fight the devil." Well, that's a losing battle because the other guy's got all the guns. Martin Luther King, Jr., took a different approach, spoonfeeding people. First, you get them listening to the Word. Then you get them singing and clapping their hands. Then, they walk down the aisle. Then, they walk out into the street. It was a mental approach to the civil rights movement, which turned out to be the most powerful one. You just can't take people who've been on their knees all their lives and put guns in their hands. It just ain't gonna work. Same goes for radio. You can't have the kind of militant talk that we had unsuccessfully at WLIB for so many years. You don't get the kind of action you need. So what can we do? We now have gospel as the thing you hang your hat on, and then we will begin to introduce the other kind of programs that will feed the mind in more secular ways.

Are the numbers improving yet?
I don't expect them to improve dramatically. It's not that kind of format. It takes a lot of work in the community to make that thing work. And it will take time.

So if you know it won't make any money, why do you hold onto WLIB? What's the emotional connection?
It's where we started. It's our roots. Also, with the evolution of radio that's going on, and with the emerging digital world, eventually there won't be a difference in the quality of AM offerings.

So you're saying WLIB can be a moneymaker in the future?
Oh, yeah.

Where do you see NABOB going in the future? Has the organization had any success over the years?
There's always been a resistance to putting money into a concerted effort to improve the advertising community for black radio. It's expensive. It requires a lot of research. Ours has been more of a political organization. We've fought battles against consolidation and battles of a political nature.

And how is that going?

Well, we've lost every battle. We've had Republican control of Congress for many years, and the first thing they did was throw out the tax certificate. Without that the number of African Americans who have owned radio stations has gone down dramatically. Also, the biggest threat to black radio right now is something called the PPM, the Personal People Meter.

This is kind of like a beeper that you wear, and it records whatever radio stations you listen to?

Right, radio stations encode their signals, so that they can get credit for having a certain number of listeners.

And that number is used in soliciting advertising.

But one of the problems with this is that the PPM records ambient sounds around you. So even though black folks listen to their radio station, we live in a white world. When we go into stores and buy clothing, there's a rock station on. When we go shopping for food, somebody else's station is on. Usually the largest stores in our communities are playing somebody else's station because they're owned by white folks. You would have to go into [black-serviced] carwashes all day to make the numbers more accurate [laughs]. So we've engaged Arbitron on this issue of undercounting black audiences, but they have been reluctant to make any changes. They've just refused to deal with the issue.

So the greatest threat to black radio comes down to advertising dollars, again.

Yeah. With the PPM, we'd be out of business.

Has any progress been made?

A few years ago, I went to the big annual advertiser's conference to speak at the luncheon. These are all the decisionmakers in the advertising world, and they get together to discuss what, I do not know. They invited me to say some words. And as I looked out into that sea of faces in that luncheon room, I said, "I'm curious as to why you invited me here. Because the problem with you guys is that there's nobody out there that looks like me."

Really!

And a woman from *USA Today* approached me. She had said she'd be wearing a black dress at the reception, and I said I'd be the black guy [laughs]. You know, and I told her that I've been told over the years by advertising agencies that black people don't fly airplanes, and we don't drive Mercedes. So I said, "I'm a Mercedes Benz–driving pilot." She put that in the article. The point is that there are all kinds of misconceptions about who we are, and they kind of prefer the stereotype. It kind of sticks with them. . . . They can't help it. Have there been changes? Yes, but they're slow to happen. And there's always some monster like the PPM that jumps up.

It seems like we're going backwards in terms of ownership.

Well, you could say that. We've been under attack by Republicans for ownership of media, and we've been undervalued by the advertisers.

Do you plan to stay in the business much longer?

No. I like radio. It has been very good to me. But there are other things that I want to do. At my age, I just don't see the need to hold on. I don't want to have a death grip on this thing.

What else would you like to do?

I've got some writing to do, and I'd like to focus on cable. The truth of it is that we, as a family, never made a whole lot of money. I'm not a millionaire.

You're not?

No.

That's surprising.

We have sixty-three shareholders, and there was some pressure to become a public company from the share ownership. So we decided to go out and buy some radio stations. I went out, and I bought clusters of radio stations in South Carolina and Mississippi, and then the radio and advertising industry went south. It became a real burden because I had just borrowed a hell of a lot of money. So that has been a struggle to overcome in the last several years. We've had to focus, and we have focused.

Have you streamlined your holdings?

Well, you can't cut your way to success, really. You have to invest. And we have done that. And it takes time for an investment to pan out. But we are now on very solid footing. We've got some syndications going; we're going to expand the nature of our product and spread that around the country. So I think it's a good time to get out. I'm not rushing to get out, but I want to leave the place in good shape. We've gone through some tough times. I've been fighting all my life.

Are you tired of the business?

No, I enjoy it. But I've been doing it for quite some time, and I don't see the need to hold on to it when there are other things I could also do, and enjoy, and actually make some money at.

Recently, Inner City sold Urban Cable in Philadelphia, to Time Warner.

Right, Urban Cable doesn't exist anymore. I sold it out of necessity because we had obligations that went beyond, and outside of, the radio business. But one of the things I plan to do is buy some more cable assets and cable systems.

I interviewed Chauncey Bailey [who was murdered in July of 2007, following this interview] and Leonard Stephens in Oakland, California. These are young entrepreneurs who are taking advantage of low-power cable opportunities. Is that an option for you?

I think it's great for them, but I'm not at the stage of the game where I want to do that kind of work. You can have some measure of success, but an awful lot of work has to go into it. For me, that's just not the kind of game I want to play.

With ongoing consolidations it doesn't seem like there are a lot of available cable systems sitting around. How do you break in?

There are a lot of markets that are available. . . . Maybe I'm interested in a system in, for example, Columbia, South Carolina. Or maybe Jackson, Mississippi. The opportunities may be smaller, but the truth is that cable is essentially a utility. Once you purchase it and maintain it, you don't have to compete with anybody, which is what I like about it.

Why do you think other black owners haven't bought more of these small systems?

I don't know. I was the last black guy in the cable business. So I don't know why it hasn't occurred to them. I just know that I can do it.

Why do you think those few African Americans who have held ownership in cable have sold?

Black folks in cable didn't last very long. I myself don't understand the rapidity with which black people abandoned cable. But they saw that the price of assets they had secured for a relatively small amount of money skyrocketed, and they saw an opportunity to take themselves to the beach. Bob Johnson sold. And in Detroit—

Don Barden, who founded the first African American–owned cable company in the country, Barden Communications, in the 1970s.

Yes, Don Barden.

He declined to be interviewed for this project.

[Laughs] I'm not surprised. He beat us out for the franchise in Detroit.

You applied?

Yes. And we applied in Washington, DC, too, and got beat out by Bob Johnson. Basically, everybody won on their home turfs. But Don Barden did something that just amazed me, and I still admire him for it [laughs]. For the city council discussions, he brought all these black ladies in, and they were all dressed in white and all saying the same things. They testified, ad nauseum, saying absolutely nothing and basically filibustered the whole thing! We had the top ratings in terms of our engineering . . . but none of that mattered. When you get beat good, you really appreciate it, and he kicked our butts good! I'm still tickled by that. I don't know where Don is now.

Las Vegas.

That's right. He's doing the casinos.

He was the first black casino owner in Las Vegas.

That's right, that's right. Yeah, he's a smart man. I like him. But all around the country people sold. Because they saw the value of the cable industry exceeding by great measure the amount of money they'd put into it. So they saw for themselves an opportunity to do something else. Cable is very interesting. Do you know how cable started?

How?

There was a guy in the wilds of Pennsylvania who had an appliance store. He was selling television sets, but nobody in that valley could receive signals. So he had the idea of putting an antenna on the hill and running a wire through it to connect those homes to signals in the outside world. That was originally called CATV, Community Antenna TV, which evolved into cable. But the value of cable has become so great because it's not merely television signals now. You have telephones, Internet service . . . it's a utility that people will pay for like they pay their mortgages or their rent. And one of the interesting things is that people don't see the value of cable in the black community. Because it's relatively cheap entertainment, the value of a cable system in the *black* community is potentially far greater than that in the white community.

It's well-documented that black people watch more television hours than non-African Americans, and we also are willing to pay more for premium cable services.

That's exactly right. But banks don't get that. My father supervised the development of cable television in Lower Manhattan, the first cable system in New York. But when he went to get financing for the development of cable in

Queens, he could not do it because he was black. We had the same problem when we were trying to get money, years earlier, for radio. I don't know how many, dozens of banks, turned us down. The only reason we got the money was because one of our shareholders, when he was a camp counselor, had saved the life of the daughter of the president of the bank.

Really!

And that's kind of ridiculous. But that really is a fact of life. It *really* did happen that way. And even then we were put in the "Urban Lending" department of that bank.

In the end, why does it matter that media is black owned?

It matters tremendously. White folks just don't see that they have a very different view of the world than we have. When I first dealt with Air America, I saw that the fellow that had the vision for it had a very good vision. He just didn't handle himself very well financially, and he made some terrible mistakes. But then, the saviors of Air America really didn't get it either. If you're going to purport to be a progressive radio network, you have to ask, "What are you being progressive about?" America is a rainbow, to take Jesse's thing. And even the people who currently run Air America don't understand that you can't take something that purports to understand the value system of America, and have everybody in charge of that vision be of one culture. But that's what they have there. And they'll never get it until they open up their doors to include folks who don't come from their culture.

They would probably point out that they have Chuck D.

Chuck D sits on their board. Chuck D is a rapper. He knows what's going on in the street. But do you see any changes going on over there because of Chuck D? Have they put anybody black on the air? The one person they have on the air is a guy who I forced them to have on by contract, Mark Reilly. He wouldn't be there now if I hadn't forced him on them, and held them to the contract.

That was part of your agreement?

Yeah. I had to be certain. I felt that they had to have some continuity [with WLIB]. And I'm glad that I did. They tried to cover him up and bury him. . . . But in any case, when they were at their lowest point I offered to give them some staff support because they didn't know the first thing about radio. They had brought television people in. Radio is not television. It's a more spontaneous medium. It is not something you structure words to all the time. And that's what they were doing, in addition to their cultural biases. So, the chairman didn't respond to my offer of help, and later on, he came back and asked me to do something for him, after midnight, around the election. I said, "Why is it that you didn't respond to my offer of support?" I wasn't charging for it. And his response to me was, "We don't want ya'll to run the radio station." Well, there you go. Just like that.

So why does black ownership matter?

If you don't own the medium you can't control the message. We don't see a news story the same way. They see a black man on the news as being automatically guilty. You know . . . it's real when Amado Diallo gets shot up. How can you shoot somebody—how many times? And you reloaded how many times? They just don't get it, and I don't know if they ever can. They can't express the events in the black community the way that we can. Because we feel it, we live here.

CHAPTER 4

WILLIAM DELFORD DAVIS

Willie Davis, seventy-two, a former NFL Super Bowl champion for the Green Bay Packers, was unlike most athletes of his day. Not only did he play in the first two Super Bowls, in 1967 and 1968, and become a member of the Pro Football Hall of Fame in 1981, but Davis also had the foresight to plan for a life after sports by attending the University of Chicago during off seasons. He was awarded his MBA in 1968, just before retiring from professional football.

In South Los Angeles, Davis went on to found the West Coast Beverage Company, a venture he quickly grew into a multimillion-dollar enterprise with a total of 126 employees. In 1976, Davis shifted gears again and founded All Pro Broadcasting, Inc., which remains a majority black-owned media company in partnership with Northwestern Mutual Life. That same year, All Pro acquired its first radio station, K-ACE in Los Angeles, a rhythm and blues and oldies format that Davis salvaged from bankruptcy and made profitable. Today, the company owns four radio stations: KCKC-AM News and Talk and KAEV-FM Urban Contemporary in San Bernardino, California; and WMCS-AM News and Talk and WLUM-FM Adult Contemporary in Milwaukee, Wisconsin.

*   *   *

Can we talk a little bit about your upbringing? Your father left the family when you were eight years old and joined the Merchant Marines. How did that impact you?

I never really developed a relationship with my dad until he was on his dying bed, in 1987. He even worked for me for the last seven years or so of his life. I used to tell him, it was just hard for me to forgive the fact that he went away and left my mom with raising us. On his deathbed, I was finally able to forgive him. He told me that one of the reasons he left was that he couldn't provide for us the kind of life that he thought a man should be able to do for his family.

What was your mother like?

Oh my God, my mother. I just loved my mother to death. Probably everything I've ever done in my life has a little bit of my mom inside of it. There was always a kind of a hidden motivation because I was doing this for more than Willie. I was doing this for me, my mother, and all the things that I wanted us to be judged on. I was the first one in my immediate family to attend and graduate from college. I went to Grambling College in Louisiana, where I was captain of the football team.

What kind of work did your mother do?

My mother was a head cook at the Texarkana Country Club, which you could imagine was a pretty good job. It was membership only, white only, for the wealthy people there. So we ate far better than most because they let her bring leftover food home. My mother also did a little catering on the side.

So she was an entrepreneur, too.

Absolutely! She was more of an entrepreneur than we even recognized at the time. You know, there were twelve in her family, as a girl, so she never knew much beyond a very poor and struggling life. But she was an excellent basketball player when she was young. She excelled at that, and she was kind of known for it. She got a high school education but never went any further. My mother wanted to go to college, and she would have gone had she been able to.

She got to see some of your successes before she died.

Yeah, she did. She passed away in 1986, so she saw me inducted into the Pro Football Hall of Fame in 1981. And when I got on my first couple of corporate boards, for the Fireman's Fund and Schlitz Malt Liquor, I called my mom to tell her. She was real quiet at first. And after a while, she said, "But honey, is it safe?" [Laughs] She didn't understand what it was. So I said, "Mom, it's like I got into the country club. Being on a board is made up of those kinda people." I said, "It's very special, Mom." Every board I was on, I was the first and the only black person.

In the mid-1970s, you got involved in radio. What sparked your interest in ownership?

A broker got in touch with me about this Inglewood station that was in bankruptcy. It had been owned by [renowned music executive and former chairman of Motown] Clarence Avant. That's the station that would later become K-ACE. It was interesting because Redd Foxx, the actor from the show *Sanford and Son*, was supposed to buy the station with a partner, but they backed out at the last minute. So, the broker called me at five o'clock on a Friday—a gentleman by the name of Cliff Gill. He said he had to report back to the bankruptcy judge on Monday. The judge was in charge of the license and equipment, and he had given Cliff a couple of months to sell the station.

The broker must have been desperate.

Yes. So I had three days to make a decision about buying the equipment and the license out of bankruptcy. I told Cliff, "Well, I've always loved radio." I mean, in the South I listened to the radio almost every day, but really, I was very uncertain because I was in the beer business. So I was president of the Urban League, at the time, and I had gone to Boston for a meeting that weekend. I was in the hotel, and I didn't want to go back to my room because I wanted to avoid Cliff's calls. So I was downstairs in the lobby, and he had me paged! He was so aggressive, and yet so positive. You know, and he was a consulting engineer, too, so he said, "Willie, if you do this, I will come to work and help you get this thing on the air." Cliff Gill. He just passed away.

If you hadn't bought the station, would it have gone to a non-minority owner?

Yes, it would have gone up for a new auction that would have been much more open. There were four or five people who were interested but no other minority applicants. This was at a time when the FCC was trying to get more blacks into broadcasting.

How much did you pay for it?

I paid $250,000 for the license and equipment, and I probably spent another $600,000 or $700,000 to get it back on the air.

That was a bargain!

Yes. Today it's worth close to $15 million.

And you made it profitable within six months.

Yes.

One of the things you did with K-ACE was you banned "gangsta rap." Why?

There was just no way I was prepared to put those songs on the air with that kind of low-class talk about females. There was rap, and it was getting a little more violent and a little more sexually explicit, but then when it went to gangsta rap, well, that was it for me. I said, "We're just going to eliminate all rap." People were worried about the record companies, but I said, "I don't care." I was embarrassed, frankly, when I heard some of it. And if I was in mixed company, I was downright uncomfortable. Did we get criticized? Yeah. Do I care? No.

I was living here in my hometown, Los Angeles, at the time, and I remember that. I was a big fan of K-ACE. You also changed formats and went to all oldies.

Yeah, yeah, we did.

Did that impact your ratings or advertiser support?

I don't think so because when we went to oldies, we were already playing to an older audience. Our listener was more twenty-five to fifty-four. Also, with advertisers, you find out real fast that whites do not want a rap-related crowd in their stores. It was interesting. I was down in San Bernardino, and I went into a place where the guy said, "Is your station the one that plays rap?" I said, "No." And he said, "Well, I should be honest with you. We don't want them in our store. We would not buy advertising with you if your station played rap."

I'm told that this is a very common response to stations with rap or urban formats.

Yeah. So Clear Channel addressed that by going to business establishments and saying, "We have seven stations in the market. And while two of them might not be stations you would normally buy, we'll give you all seven if you give us a certain high percentage of the advertising budget." Well, that has been devastating in some quarters to the small owner.

You have always made it clear that athletes and entertainers are role models, whether they want to be or not.

Yes, we are. There's no question in my mind that if we could turn back the clock on some of this bad behavior, we would be in a better place. The kind of things you see with some of the athletes today . . . it's outrageous.

You have more conservative values.

I never realized I was conservative until I started looking at what I rejected.

Why did you sell K-ACE?

I sold in 1995 when the FCC was beginning to let all the big operators buy up whole groups of radio stations. I decided that in a place like Los Angeles, if you only had one signal, you were probably going to be in trouble.

So it was because of the impact of FCC policy changes.

Well, it was because I believed it would become more difficult to be successful because of consolidation by the big stations.

But didn't that consolidation happen because of FCC policies that allowed big owners to get bigger?

Yeah, yeah, I guess you're right. And you know what was interesting, before that thing started, they had six black-oriented stations in Los Angeles, and three of them were owned by African Americans. As consolidation started to happen, you had what had previously been general-market stations coming in, buying up urban stations and throwing a heck of a lot more resources in it. So it was a matter of doing something before the thing caved in on you. I sold K-ACE to Cox Cable for $11 million and ended up buying two other stations. . . . Not too many people know this, but Stevie Wonder [legendary rhythm and blues artist and composer, and owner of KLJH-FM in Los Angeles] wanted to buy another station. Before I sold K-ACE, we were very close to doing a deal together. We had several conversations, and I believe that, together, we probably could have been okay.

Why didn't it work out?

What happened is that with all the changes, four of those other stations that were black-oriented just went away. So all at once Stevie had a greater chance to survive without the competition. KJLH kind of had the dance to themselves for a little while. But now it's gotten much more competitive with several of the big operators coming back into the market.

You've recently switched to an all-talk format at your Milwaukee station, WMCS-AM (1290). Why?

One thing that we wanted to do there was to be able to address all of the horrible issues in Milwaukee: the teen pregnancies, the crime. We're deeply involved in trying to be of some support on this teen pregnancy problem in Milwaukee. When I first heard that Milwaukee was the number-one city for black teen pregnancies, I called my station manager, Don Rosette, and said, "We've got to do something about this." I didn't think we would get eighteen- to thirty-four-year-olds, but at least we would be able to talk to the parents and the adults that could possibly have some control over the situation. So the whole purpose for going talk was to really address community issues.

So, you as the owner were directly responsible for initiating an educational campaign on your station to address the problem of teen pregnancy?

Yeah, I surely was the one, yes. And I've been involved with some fund-raising efforts. I just felt that there was no way I could stay in radio and seriously believe that I was giving something back if I didn't address that situation.

Do you know if it's had an impact?

I think Planned Parenthood would say that, yes, we have been of some help.

Your motto for WMCS is "Community First." Do you think it matters to the community that you are black owned?

Well, when I'm out at events and I see people, they're always thanking me for the stations. We just finished an event in Milwaukee for the Mother Katherine Daniels Center, where I was their first honoree for the Lifetime Achievement Award. We raised $460,000 at that event to support their efforts with the school and with education.

And you have a scholarship fund.

Yes, we have the Willie D. Davis Scholarship situation, and we've raised and supported 350 kids with over $750,000 during the last probably ten years. Many of them have gone on to black colleges.

Let's talk about football again for a moment because I know there was a time when you wanted to be an NFL owner, and you went through that whole elaborate interview process for a deal that ultimately did not pan out. What happened?

Well, some friends were trying to make an NFL situation a reality in Memphis in the late 1980s. I was interested, but the obligations and the liability with a football team could scare you to death. Back then, the television money wasn't as big, so you could all at once end up paying millions. But for the people with money and ego, they were going to write it off against their other enterprises, and, frankly, that's what I said, too. I said I could use some of the tax credit to support other things. I thought we were very close to the Memphis situation. I was disappointed when we didn't get that deal.

You would have been the first African American NFL owner.

Yes, they were interested in getting diversity into the league. But even today there are maybe just a couple of minority owners with very small shares in franchises. Actually, I don't know, as I sit here today, one black owner in football.

On the other hand, you turned down NFL coaching offers.

Well, I had gone back to the University of Chicago and gotten an MBA and the corporate job offers I was getting were so interesting. So I said, "I made all this investment in my education and my dream of being an entrepreneur. Why would I just jump at coaching now?" But I tell you, frankly, if I had envisioned that it could have led to head coaching, I probably would have gone another way.

There were no black head coaches in the NFL back then.

You're absolutely right. Black head coaches only go back maybe seven, eight years. But I can tell you, to this day, I still think of what it would have been like if I had gone into coaching.

Do you have some regrets about that?

Yeah, I have some regrets. Art Modell [owner of the Cleveland Browns] called me maybe in the early 1980s about coaching. I said, "Gee, you know, I'm in this business thing now." And he said, "Well, why don't you let us buy the business and you can come coach?" That was one of the worst nights of my life. I suffered thinking about it because coaching probably would have been my first choice. But I was doing well in business, and it was also satisfying.

Did you think you couldn't go as far in coaching as you could go in business?

If there had been examples of black head coaches, I'm sure I would have thought more positively about going in.

I read that Johnny Roland [former running back with the St. Louis Cardinals and coach on five NFL teams] said that he left the game in 1978 to run a radio station because he didn't see enough opportunities for advancement in coaching.

Johnny was a great football player. You're telling me something that I did not know myself. But there were a lot of players that were coming out of the game and trying to find a career, and what people don't realize is that my last year playing football I only made $50,000. At the time, I thought this was big-time money, but in the beer business I was getting a salary of $125,000 my first year! The truth is that there are an awful lot of great opportunities outside of sports, but that side of life is really understated.

Yes. You once said that sports were a "temporary joy," and that sports were not going to fix the fact that "we are not paying our teachers." Let's get back to the media. In 1994, you partnered with music producer Quincy Jones, television journalist Geraldo Rivera, and Soul Train *creator Don Cornelius on a minority-owned company called Qwest Broadcasting to buy television stations.*

Yeah. Quincy was the main individual, and his people from Time Warner were supporting the effort. He had some ownership of a station in New Orleans, and they came up with the idea of buying an Atlanta station as well, WATL.

Time Warner knew that if they sold to a minority group, they would get the tax credit.

No question. And I was kind of given the role of representing Qwest in the financial management of the situation. To have that opportunity was really special, and it meant as much to me as anything. We had absolute fantastic success in Atlanta and a reasonable amount of success in New Orleans. I often wondered what would have happened had we not sold. I still think we'd be doing pretty well.

You would have had the New Orleans station during Hurricane Katrina.

I have thought about that many times. You know, I was born near Lisbon, Louisiana.

Do you think about how your news coverage of the storm might have been different if Qwest had still owned the station?

There's no question. I mean, from day one, we were bound and determined to be the best at serving the community, and I think we did that. I think that's why we had such amazing success.

Why did you sell?

Well, that one was somewhat predetermined. When we went into the deal, Tribune Broadcasting, which was the other partner with us and had 45 percent ownership, had an option to buy us out in five years. So either way, in five years something was probably going to happen. Now you ask, "Why didn't we attempt to buy them out?" Well, Tribune paid us a pretty good buck to get out.

You had other ideas about what you wanted to do with the money.

Yes. I took part of that money and retired all of my radio debt. Because I had decided that I wanted to have this business not owing a nickel to anybody. So two years ago I accomplished that. Why was that important? Some of the better business people would say debt is not bad, you just manage it. But for me it was almost like when we were in that first NFL championship game in Chicago, and I was standing there holding the trophy. I said, "Of all the people in the world that play this game, the Green Bay Packers are the best."

You compared not having any debt to being number one.

Yeah. It was like freedom. When I owned the beverage company, I owned it 100 percent. And when you own something 100 percent, you don't report to anybody.

What do you think about the future of black media ownership?

Black media ownership went away big time with all these stations being bought out by the Clear Channels and the Infinities of the world. And you could have forecasted this would happen with no federal guidelines or rules in place. The sale of WAWA AM-FM in Milwaukee went through [to me] on the minority tax credit.

And now those policies that encouraged minority ownership are gone.

Clear Channel literally went to the largest cities in the country and bought up the maximum number of stations there, sometimes seven or eight stations in one market. So now people are saying, "Well, gee, that seems to go against the public interest."

How can the few black owners who are left survive?

I think maybe the churches might be the most likely participants in the future. Because, many times, they're committed to finding a home for their religious programming. And they can get the money to finance these things.

Even Radio One is facing challenges.

Yes. In Los Angeles, KKBT "The Beat" recently flipped its format. It's now Beat 100, so they're doing a lot of R&B. That will definitely affect Stevie Wonder's station. It's going to be interesting to see what happens next.

CHAPTER 5

FRANK WASHINGTON

Frank Washington, fifty-nine, is an important player in the story of minority media ownership, even referring to himself as the "alpha and omega" of the FCC's Minority Ownership Policy. As the man who played a large role in initiating the original legislation in the 1970s, Washington explains that he also brought it down in one fell swoop, with one deal gone bad, twenty years later. Unlike many of the owners in this book, Washington—an attorney and entrepreneur—is less interested in the content of programming than he is in the business of the media industry.

Born in Washington, DC, and raised outside of New York City, in Rockland County, Washington says that he had no exposure to business growing up.

* * *

Can you talk a little bit about your upbringing. . . . What did your parents do for a living?

Both my parents graduated from high school. My father was a blue collar worker in a paper factory. My mother was a secretary. I was the first person in my family to get a four-year degree, much less a graduate degree in law. I'm an anomaly in so many ways, it's not even funny.

How did you become interested in media?

When I was at Yale, I wrote a piece that was published in the *Law Journal* called "Community Ownership of Cable Television." It was the early 1970s, and there was a lot of promise that cable was going to be a new avenue for unheard voices. I had worked with the Urban League in Connecticut on a project involving cable franchises, which had not yet been built and were actually being warehoused by a bunch of politicians who were just kind of sitting on them, waiting to sell. Then, I got involved in a Ford Foundation project that looked at trying to change some of the limitations on public access to the airwaves.

It was a fellowship?

Well, I was hired as a consultant on the Urban Communications Project, which was funded by the Ford Foundation. Keep in mind, I was in law school when this was going on, and part of that work actually involved interviewing various FCC commissioners. Basically, there was a law firm that was focused on trying to push the FCC to give greater access to minorities in the airwaves.

Were people still pushing for broadcast, or had they started to look at cable, too, in the early 1970s?

Well, it was supposed to be focused on broadcasting, but because of the Urban League project I had been involved in, I was aware of cable. Back then, it was still basically just retransmitting from broadcast television. You know, most of the cable systems were lucky to have thirteen or fourteen channels. So it wasn't the way it is today. The focus was still primarily on broadcasting.

How did you become interested in working for the FCC?

Well, I became interested in communications. I was hired by a law firm, Arnold & Porter, which has a long history of working with Washington bureaucracy. At that time, they had a very small communications department, which turned out to be a big advantage to me because, unlike the big law firms today where you're the fifth associate on a deal, I got to work directly with clients. The variety of projects included everything from representing the commissioner of baseball to working with small broadcasters and cable systems. After about three years in this law firm, a friend approached me about joining President Carter's White House as a consultant on communications policy.

Why do you think you were chosen?

Carter had a big vote from the black community, and there were a number of black leaders who were pressuring him to do something specific with regard to minority ownership. At the time, less than 1 percent of the media was owned by minorities. So Carter had made this commitment, and, in 1977, I was brought in to focus on that.

It was in that context that I came up with the idea for the Minority Tax Certificate.

That was your idea?

It was. Carter had a strong inclination to make changes in the tax code. That was part of his platform, and it was clear to me that some sort of a tax credit would have a huge impact in advancing minority ownership.

How did you come up with the idea?

I was aware of a procedure called the tax certificate, which originally had been put into place by Congress in the 1950s when the FCC started forcing divestitures of stations that were owned by large newspaper companies. There was a big concern back then about consolidation and that the media was becoming monopolized. So they forced a number of groups to spin off their radio and television stations. In order to take some of the sting out of that, they created what was called the tax certificate, which basically operated as a tax deferral. It's similar to what the deferral would be on your house if you sold it. You have a period of time within which, if you buy another home, you can avoid paying the tax by basically rolling it into the new property. I was aware of the tax certificate, but when I looked at it, I realized it was written so generally that the FCC could basically decide minority ownership was in the public interest, and the tax certificate could be used in that way. The beauty of this is that it was a win-win for everybody.

What was your first step in trying to get it implemented?

I went to the National Association of Broadcasters, which had given a lot of lip service to the idea of minority ownership, but hadn't really done anything. In fact, I asked them if they would be willing to petition the FCC to put it into place. Even though I was working at the White House, I thought it would carry more force if the industry itself came out in favor of this. So they did. Toward the end of 1977, I was hired by the chairman of the FCC, Charles Ferris, as his legal assistant. He had been the legislative assistant to the head of the Senate for a number of years and had just been nominated by Carter to be chairman of the FCC. So I went over to the FCC and in that capacity basically wrote the Minority Ownership Policy Statement that created the tax certificate.

Right, and the certificate worked together with the distress sale policy.

Yes. The tax certificate and the distress sale policy were the two pieces of this Minority Ownership Policy Statement. And that went on until 1996, when Congress retroactively repealed the section of the tax code that it was all based on. Prior to that repeal, the percentage of minority-owned broadcasting stations quadrupled. They went from less than 1 percent to over 3 percent. So it clearly had, by far, more impact than anything else that had been done before or since.

Why was it repealed?

I was kind of the alpha and the omega of the tax certificate. In 1995, I had done a deal involving Viacom's cable systems. It was a $2.3 billion deal and would have been the largest deal ever done by a minority. It certainly would have been the largest one using the tax certificate. Unfortunately, it coincided with the Republican takeover of Congress and, if you recall, one of their platforms was basically doing away with preferences being given to minorities. This deal was not a "preference" in the classic sense because the seller was getting benefits. It wasn't like something was being taken away from an existing broadcaster. But very astutely, from a political standpoint, the Republicans saw the size of the deal and immediately focused on it as a way to make their political case. I spent about four months lobbying with a number of people to avoid this. But they did it in such a skillful way that even though Bill Clinton was president, they tied it to another piece of legislation, which he felt obligated not to veto.

The health care bill for small business owners.

Right. We almost got it knocked down in the Senate, but I ran into a problem with Bob Dole. He was running for president and found himself in a situation where he felt he had to support it. Even though we initially had the votes from Republicans in the finance committee to get it knocked down, he forced a party line vote because he didn't want to look like he was any less conservative than the people he was running against at the time. I made a last-ditch effort to try to get it vetoed by Clinton, but, as I said, they tied it to a health insurance bill, and he didn't feel like he could veto health insurance. So that was the end of that. Not only did it kill my deal, but it killed the tax certificate.

How did you feel about that?

How do you think I felt? It was pretty classic Jim Crow kind of behavior. The irony was that the sale went through anyway, and the buyer got a tax write-off for it. They just used a different section of the code. So the only difference was that no minority was involved in the deal. When the tax certificate was no longer a factor, that took away all the leverage I had. The parties that were interested, Viacom as the seller and TCI as the buyer, just wound up doing the deal directly. John Malone [of Liberty Media, formerly known as TCI] was my backer when we had the certificate. But being the very smart guy that he is he was able to find another section of the tax code that gave him a deferral anyway.

What did you do next?

When I left the FCC in 1981, I was fortunate to get a job working for the *Tribune* in Los Angeles, which was owned by the *Los Angeles Times* and also owned cable systems. I went to work for the cable portion of the company, which was viewed as new media at the time. They were trying a whole lot of new things, and they felt they needed somebody with some Washington experience. So I spent three years working initially for the cable company and then in a project called video text, which was a precursor to the Internet. That was how I met the McLatchie people, and they hired me in 1984 to run all their non-newspaper operations here in Sacramento, which included cable, broadcast radio, as well as some computer-driven information services. To make a long story short, I got an enormous amount of experience in all those areas. I hired [conservative radio talk show host] Rush Limbaugh here, if you can believe that, before he was nationally known.

Did you know he would become so controversial?

No idea. I mean the guy was a hit. He was going to be able to be a personality, but nobody had any idea what he was destined to become. Believe me, I would have gotten a piece of his action if I had any idea.

I mean politically, did he take these staunch conservative positions back then?

While there were people who complained about him and all of that, I saw him as someone who truly had potential as an entertainer.

How did you begin to own media?

I got a lot of experience at McLatchie, but their primary interest was newspapers. So I suggested that they sell all the non-newspaper portions of the company, recognizing that was going to do away with my own position. My hope was that I would be able to buy some of the stuff that they sold off. In fact, I did attempt to buy some of the radio stations, but it didn't quite work out. So my thought was if I'm going to do this again, I'm going to make sure that I participate in the ownership. I'm going to get a part of it. So I basically liquidated everything I had: my pension, my house, and I spent two years looking for deals. The first deal I came across involved cable systems.

Which was that?

Well, we bought a bunch of stuff. The first deal was with [former Washington Redskins owner] Jack Kent Cook, who had a bunch of cable systems. Myself and a partner, Leo Henfrey, cut a deal where we got a portion of his cable holdings through a consortium deal. I used the tax certificate, and we bought other systems as we went along. Our largest market was in Tucson, and we had a bunch of stuff around Nashville and Georgia.

What was the name of the cable system?

It was called Robin Cable Systems. And we didn't buy all the systems; we just bought some of them. Between 1988 and 1996, we bought systems with about a half a million subscribers. And throughout that period I recognized that the industry was consolidating very rapidly, which was why we attempted to buy the Viacom cable systems, which was like a million subscribers. When that deal got blown up by Congress, I recognized I was pretty much out of cable. So my partners bought me out of the deal. This was 1996, and that was the year I started buying radio stations. I bought four stations from a company that later got rolled up and became part of Clear Channel.

Which were those?
Well, there was a station in Delaware and several other stations in the New York area.

I'm just curious, what kind of formats did these stations have and why did you choose them?
I chose them because I could get them at a price that made sense. I don't care about the formats. I mean, to some degree it doesn't matter. If you can change the format and get a bigger share of the market, then that's something you would do. But I bought them because I had a special inside deal, frankly.

Were they AM or FM?
They were all FM.

Was there anything unusual about the formats?
No, and my focus was the deal itself. The seller had a problem with the FCC, and it was going to force them to sell the stations. I was able to help them with the problem in a way where I got control of the station, and they provided the financing.

The four stations had the same owner.
Yes, Capstar.

And they're pretty much out of it now?

Yeah, it was rolled up into Clear Channel. And at the same time, in 1996, I was CEO of a newspaper publishing company, and also having four radio stations report to me, which led me very quickly to conclude this was a bit of an overload. I had known a guy named Frank Osborne from years before and had talked to him about trying to do radio deals. So I approached him about the idea of he and I getting together to do a rollup of radio stations. And that's what happened. I rolled the stations into a group and sold them in 2002 for about $3 million to Cumulus.

Why did you sell?

Because somebody made us an offer we couldn't refuse. Later, we created Quantum Communications, which has about thirty stations today.

And what kind of ownership do you have in Quantum?

Well, I'm not free to discuss that. I've invested money, and I have a parity interest. I'm more aligned with management than as an investor. I'm not involved in operations on a day-to-day basis, but as a board member I'm pretty heavily involved in what goes on, mostly dealing with transactions.

Were any of the companies you have been involved with minority owned?

Well, when we first bought the four stations from Capstar Broadcasting, I controlled that. I didn't have a majority interest, but I controlled the operations. I also was the only general partner in the cable channels . . . but didn't have majority ownership. You know, for most people there's no way to be a majority owner because you have to have an investor, and since investors invariably put up most of the money, there's no way you're going to wind up with a majority of the interest. Bob Johnson [founder of BET] got a sweet deal with TCI where he was able to keep a majority position in 1980. But today with prices as they are, you're always going to have an investor somewhere putting up most of the money. You'd be lucky to have control.

Does minority ownership matter in your opinion?

For groups like the National Association of Black-Owned Broadcasters, that's a big deal. From my standpoint, I recognize that to be in a position to do anything at all, I'm going to have to play ball with other people. Of course it matters as far as how much you walk away with at the end.

It sounds like you're saying that it matters from a business perspective, but not necessarily from a social or political perspective.

Well, I look at these things as business opportunities first, and social realities second. It's pretty dangerous to think you're going to buy something for social reasons. That's usually a prescription for losing a lot of money. But having said that, the reality is that focusing on the minority arena has generally turned out to be pretty good approach. I'll give you an example. I just started a TV station here in Sacramento two years ago. It's focused on foreign language television, with as much local programming as we can get. I bought a low-powered television station because I didn't think the business model would support buying a full-powered TV station in Sacramento. If you can find one, you're talking $30 or $40 million as a minimum, and I didn't think serving the Mong and Punjabi and Chinese market in this area would support that kind of a purchase price. So I bought a low-powered station for a million and a half bucks. The key was that there was nobody else really serving this market on a local basis. There were a lot of satellite signals focused on those various ethnic groups, but my feeling was that people weren't going to see themselves on a signal coming from New York.

So by offering more local programming for ethnic groups you've found an untapped niche in Sacramento.

Yes, and low-power stations, unlike full-power television, are not required to be carried by cable systems. But in this case, the local operator, Comcast, wanted to be competitive with the satellite guys, and they realized they could do this if they carried programming that was different from the satellite programming. So Comcast agreed to carry us not only here in Sacramento but also on their cable systems in Fresno, Stockton, Modesto, Sacramento, and Marysville, which is basically all the way up to Chico, and the entire

central valley of California. As far as I know, it is unprecedented for a low-powered station to be carried that widely,
and there is a fairly large and diverse ethnic community
covered by that footprint. My point is that business strategy
is focused on finding underserved markets wherever they
might be, and it's more often than not that minority markets are underserved.

*Right. So are you the majority owner in this low-power station
in Sacramento?*

No, I brought in an investor to back us. The investor
happens to be a black firm, but that's just the way it
worked out. It could have just as easily have been a non-
minority investor.

*I read a statement a while back where you said you thought the
Minority Ownership Policies were now outdated. Do you still
feel that way?*

I don't know that I said they were outdated. I mean, I
got away with the Minority Tax Certificate because
nobody was paying attention. And look what I did, I
caught my own pass. I came up with the idea, then went
over to the FCC and wrote the policy statement. Part of
the reason it worked is because I didn't have to go though
Congress, which is a dysfunctional entity that's incapable
of doing anything right, in my opinion.

So the policy worked.

I think the tax certificate served its purpose. It drew the
best and the brightest of the minority community to the

industry. You had a whole lot of very smart people getting involved. At the same time, it got the non-minority community to understand this was an area that needed to be given serious consideration. So, I think from that standpoint it did its job. Even if Congress did pass something today, I guarantee you it would be so limited that it would be useless. The only people who would be able to use it would be people doing very small deals. And in today's reality, small deals aren't going to get you very far. But I do think there are other things that could be done to foster more minority ownership.

Like what?

Well, policies involving low-powered television, for example. Making it so low power has the same carriage rights on cable as a full-powered station. That would change the ability of those stations to be more competitive. The only reason I was able to get on here was because of my relationship with Comcast and having the right kind of programming to get Comcast to agree to carry it. [Giving low power the same access as full power] would result in a lot more creative content oriented towards minorities. In addition, it would give minorities an entry because, frankly, it always comes back to money. It's very difficult to attract investors because the majority of these investment firms are not interested in smaller deals.

And so, today, do you agree with the goals of NABOB?

Well, I'm certainly in favor of it, and I definitely think it's an area that continues to be underserved.

Who do you admire in the media business? Was there someone you looked to as a role model?

You know, I don't know that I can answer that question off the top of my head . . . I've created my own model. There weren't too many people doing what I did. I think the person that I could probably point to was a guy named Herb Wilkins who was the head of a private equity firm called Sincom. He was smart enough to be out there anticipating the Minority Tax Certificate. In fact, it was one of his deals that I actually used when I wrote the policy statement. His deal was sitting at the FCC at the time, and we were able to use it as proof to the pudding.

So, he was a visionary.

He's continued to be ahead of his time. His firm has done some cutting-edge things. They had a lot to do with Bob Johnson. They had a lot to do with Radio One. There are a number of Spanish-language entities that they were involved in. So they've done a good job of anticipating trends.

You don't hear his name much.

Well, that's right. And that's a reflection on him. He's a businessman. He's not interested in getting in front of the camera, and I think there's something to be said for that kind of reserve.

CHAPTER 6

DOROTHY EDWARDS BRUNSON

Dorothy Brunson, sixty-nine, is an inspirational figure for minority women trying to break into the closed world of media ownership. She was one of the first African American women to own a television station and the very first to own a radio station. And these are just two of her many accomplishments. In 1969, prior to these ventures, she was cofounder of the first black-owned advertising agency on Madison Avenue, which was started with just $25,000 in Small Business Administration loans together with her business partner, Howard Saunders. Today, Brunson continues to work as an independent consultant in Baltimore, Maryland.

Unassuming in appearance and manner, Brunson gives one the sense that she is a formidable businesswoman, with a sharp sense of markets, audiences, and consumer behavior. Ever since she was a girl, she says, she has wanted to be wealthy. While some minority entrepreneurs minimize the importance of generating wealth, and privilege the idea of working for a larger social or political cause, Brunson spoke openly and unabashedly about her desire to become, first and foremost, rich.

*   *   *

How did you get involved in radio?

When I first moved away from home at age eighteen, in 1956, I lived with five roommates, all of us trying to be actors. We studied acting at the Y on 145th Street in Harlem. Billy Dee Williams was in our class. I thought I would go into entertainment and be like Lena Horne. Can't sing a lick, but I was going to wear these elegant dresses and be rich. I thought that was the pathway to make money. My ultimate goal was always to make money. I stayed in it for a year and a half, and then I decided we weren't eating. So I said no way!

That's when you went to college.

Yes, but I didn't have enough money to stay there. So I came back to New York and started working. Eventually, I got a degree from CUNY in accounting and finance.

What was your first job in media?

There was a gentleman named Egmont Sonderling, a radio personality who had a foreign language program in Hebrew and Yiddish. He had a station in Oak Park, Illinois, that never made a dime. So he turned it into an all-black format, and the station went from making no money to making millions of dollars. He got an epiphany. He said, "Okay, if it worked here, why not try it somewhere else?" So he came to New York and bought this station way out on the island that had no real signal into the city, WWRL. It was an awful signal . . . because of the southern tip of Long Island. Back then, they converted stations with bad signals to "ethnic radio," with broadcasts in foreign languages like Greek, Hebrew, and Russian, and then they also created a block of time for blacks. So, Sonderling put foreign language programming on the weekends and turned Monday through Friday into all-black. We put on "Dr. Jive" [laughs]. Sonderling needed someone who had an accounting and advertising background. Since I had worked in the accounting department of a manufacturing company, I got a job with him making $17,000, which was more than many professionals at that time.

Why did he pay you so much?

Well, I later found out I was making less than everyone else there. . . . But when I started at the station, Sonderling was a Hungarian refugee and his concepts of civil rights and black Americans were not as embedded as they would become later. To him, I was not a black person in the traditional sense. I was someone he could use to be successful. I was the only black person at that station for about five years, and I was given a lot of opportunities to do things because he was in Chicago. I didn't have a clue how to do them—

But you figured it out.

I had a sense of how to solve problems, and I think that comes from being poor. One of the things we had to do was convince advertisers to buy time on the station. Our salespeople were predominantly white. So as I began to go out, I began to hear comments that they made about the black community. I was the new guy on the block: black and female. So there were a lot of levels to fight through. I had to just wait for moments. But I learned. I learned.

What did you learn?

I learned to basically counteract what they were saying in a real delicate kind of way. And I began to do the research because Nielsen didn't do anything with blacks back then, nor did [the audience research company] Arbitron. You gotta remember that up until that time you had WLIB in Harlem, and there had never been any competition for them. So, when we went on the air, we wanted to be more competitive. I wanted to be the best.

If there was no market research, how did you study and learn?

Instinct. Arbitron would measure the market and then you would see us at the very bottom of the twenty-station market. You know, Westinghouse was getting a forty rating, and we were getting a two. Well, that's interesting. So I began to cull that information. And then as I listened to the salesmen and thought, "Okay, they're saying this. That's not true." And over a two-year period, I began to disprove what they were saying through research, and instinct, and learning the patterns of how to write a proposal, and how to sell a client. Learning how to take data and manipulate it. I'll never forget, the first time it happened was with the Schaeffer Beer account. These are just moments in life you never forget. Schaeffer Beer was spending about $50,000 a year on WWRL. And I had to go out. It was not my client, but I went out with them. I'll never forget. And so the guy, the salesperson is talking . . . and there were some racist comments like, "Black people eat more of this and drink more beer" and all of this. And for them it wasn't racist, it was just fact. And they looked at me and said, "Dorothy, what do you think?" And I had to say something. You know. I guess there are always three or four minds that you have at that moment. So I think I got this guy here. I can't insult him, and I've got to deliver this account. So I answered. I don't remember what I said. I just remember how I felt about it. I felt that I answered without being insulting, but yet, giving information. And after that, six months later, Schaeffer Beer became my account. We became buddies.

Do you feel like you corrected the perceptions?

Indirectly. I didn't do it overtly, because I would have been dead. The sales guys would have made it hell for me. They made it hell for me, anyhow. They wouldn't give me paperwork on time. I had to send reports every Friday on what the sales were, what the income was, what the projections were, what were our expenses, what did we need to break even. And those guys would deliberately not give them to me.

Because you were black.

Yeah. Black and female. It was such a horror. They used to say things that were derogatory. Like, "Yeah, let's get on top of it. And let's get on top of her, too."

Right.

You get all kinds of things. But those years taught me.

You stayed at that station from 1962 to 1969, during which time you also married and had two sons, Daniel and Edward.

Yes. It was a late marriage because I really almost didn't want to be married [laughs]. But my mother and my aunt said "Women get married." We're divorced but still very good friends.

In 1969, you left WWRL and cofounded the first black advertising agency on Madison Avenue.

Yes, we were in *Newsweek* in 1969. They wouldn't rent the office to us because we were black, so we sent our good friend Saul Harrison, a Jewish guy. Saul went and got the lease and brought it back to us and we signed it. The following Monday, these two black people walked in, and they almost died [laughs]. The janitor, who was black, had showed us the space. We had to literally sneak in at night to look at it. After about a month they calmed down.

Your advertising company created the famous Schlitz Malt Liquor bull.

Yeah, we had the bull. We had Cutty Sark. We had R. J. Reynolds tobacco.

Today, we talk about how tobacco and alcohol companies have historically targeted minorities in their advertising. Did that bother you?

Yeah. We actually created a brand of cigarettes called Shamba that never came to market, but it was specifically for blacks. We were naïve. There was no evidence, and at that time no awareness, of the evils of cigarettes. It was just something that nobody thought about. People smoked Camels and Marlboros. And we wanted to make sure that black people had their brands because the awareness of the whole black experience was something that we were pushing as well. When we created Shamba, it had a Benin statue on the design, and it was really a great image with the name and the logo and the colors. The whole concept was black, red, and green.

Why did you leave advertising?

Howard Saunders and I were two different animals. I came from a mother who worked nights so she could get us off to school during the day. Howard went to Howard University and played classical piano. He had more of a cultural bent. Our work ethics were different. Howard took clients to big lunches; I didn't believe in that. So I took my share of the company and left. I started buying real estate. He stayed, and after a year he was out of business.

You were generating $1.5 million within your first year there. How did you do it?

The media is so intangible that you need someone there to give it a vision because you really are selling emotions and concepts and ideas. You're selling what you think people want to do, think, and feel. If you don't keep that awareness at the forefront of whatever you're doing, you're not going to win. I've been successful because I understood how to meet the maximum number of people, at the optimum time.

After that, you were one of the original fifty-eight black investors who bought Inner City Broadcasting, the landmark company founded by Percy and Pierre Sutton, who are also in this book. Other African American investors included civil rights leaders, educators, and entertainers, such as the Reverend Jesse Jackson, the Reverend Carl McCall, Dr. Benjamin Watkins, Billy Taylor, Roberta Flack, and Hal Jackson.

Yes. Inner City purchased WBLS and WLIB in New York. But the previous owners took all of their advertising with them the day the station was sold. Before we bought the station it had $1.5 million worth of sales. The day we bought it, it had $186,000. There was nothing there. No money to pay the bank, the bills, or the employees.

The ownership plan was very political. It came at the height of "Black Power" and movements toward economic empowerment.

Yes, in those days Adam Clayton Powell, Jr. [U.S. Congressman from 1945–1971], represented the West Indian side in Harlem. And then Percy Sutton [borough president of Manhattan from 1966–1977] and Charlie Rangel [U.S. Congressman 1971–present] and those guys came along, and they all had a lot of power. What I had a problem with was that while [the Suttons] were busy doing political shows, nobody got paid. There were no salaries. Except light and gas, there was not a person being paid. The bank hadn't been talked to. Nobody knew what the heck had been going on. Chemical Bank gave us the loan, but a year or two later, no one had even called the bank, or sent them any money. And the guy at the bank couldn't attack the borough president of Manhattan, Percy Sutton. It was this little guy at the bank that I remember best. I think he must have lost all his hair and his nerves. I remember him because I had never seen a white guy on such edge in my life! He was always on pins and needles. Because it was like a million and a half we owed at first, and then it was another million. So that was two and a half million dollars. In those days, they just didn't lend that kind of money to black people.

The station wasn't making payments on its loan?

Not a dime. So the guy at the bank actually quit, you know, after about a year. So Pierre Sutton asked if I would come and talk with them, which was a subtle way of saying would I come in for a job interview. So I went in. And they asked me, "Are you going to have any more children?" I'll never forget that question. That was very chagrining. After about three months and much prayer I took the job, but I really was not excited about it. Not at all.

Why did you take it?

In the 1970s, [the Suttons and their friends] represented political power in New York. Anything that benefited the black community went through them.

When you left, revenues were $22 million, the company owned seven stations, and its estimated value was more than $60 million. And yet, you're almost never credited for your role in making Inner City a success. Does that bother you?

It used to.

You turned WLIB around and made it profitable.

Yes, the first thing I did was got rid of the union. We had no money to pay them, first of all. And they had this awful clause in the contract. I looked at the clause and laid them all off. By that time, I knew I could do everything in the station myself. And I brought one of the guys, a Jewish guy, Mark, who was with me at WWRL. I called him my rabbi. He was, you know, one of the good guys there, and he taught me sales. So I brought him with me and made him head of sales. And I brought in a guy named Bob Schuster, who was a Russian immigrant. He didn't have a degree or anything, and he was an old man, but he was an engineer, bar none. And he did it the old way; he did it well. It was a good black-and-white team.

You were heavily criticized.

Oh God, yes! I was in every union paper. There were all kinds of attacks. I was tired. I mean, I was being attacked, and I couldn't do anything about it because I had to look at the greater good. You're put in a position where you really have to just walk a very thin, narrow path.

It would be hard to have the whole community thinking you're not for them. Has it ever gotten to you?

No. Because, you know, I'm in the midst of battle. I've been attacked. But I have done some devious things, too. One of the things I did when I was with Sonderling at WWRL was, we had no blacks on the air. We had white disc jockeys. I wanted to get black disc jockeys. And so there was a group in New York called Fight Back; rabble rousers. So I had the guy come out and picket the station. We planned the whole thing! He'd come and picket the station for weeks. I even let them do a little shoving. So my boss was getting very worried about the advertisers, and he said to me, "What are we going to do?" I said: "Well, let me go out and see if I can negotiate with them." That went on for about two weeks. Finally I said, "They're not leaving until we hire our first black announcer." And that's how I got blacks on the air.

Really!

So you claim that moment. But I had, at that point, a woman who was my secretary, a black woman. She was about fifty-five and had graduated from typing school. Marie. Everything that I did, Marie went back and told my boss. I found out about six months in. She was of a time when it was almost alien to have a black person in charge. So I fired her. And then I got—you know Jim Brown, the football player—his first wife became my secretary. Henrietta Brown. She was a young black woman. Fiery, and a college graduate.

After putting in your time with Inner City and at WLIB, you founded Brunson Communications in 1979 and became the first African American woman to buy your own radio station.
   Yes.

Your first station was WEBB-AM in Baltimore.
   Yes, the previous owner was ["Godfather of Soul"] James Brown. He lost it in a bankruptcy proceeding because of back taxes and mismanagement. It's a wonder he even has an estate left. He lost all three of his radio stations.

In 1982, you bought WIGO in Atlanta for $800,000, and the following year, WBMS in Wilmington, NC, which you later sold to purchase a full-power TV station, WGTW Channel 48 whose call letters stood for "Good Television to Watch." How did people respond to your ambition?
   People laughed. They said Philadelphia is the fourth-largest market. You'll never be able to do this. So they all just pitied me and loaned me their equipment. This was 1992. Four or five years later, I was taking their accounts.

But your programming did not necessarily focus on African Americans. It focused on seniors.
   Well, Philadelphia has the second- or third-largest senior population in the country. So, if I've got ABC, CBS, and Fox all going for the age eighteen to forty-nine market and spending millions of dollars to promote that,

then it's dumb for me to go for eighteen to forty-nine. You've got to study the program and look for the holes. On Friday and Saturday nights when they kind of gave it away, we did *New York Undercover*, and we got the eighteen to forty-four. And in the mornings, I ran health tips for seniors and stuff like *Matlock* and *Streets of San Francisco*. So it wasn't a black-programmed station. It was a general-market station that happened to have a tinge of blackness.

You were criticized again.

Well, African Americans always say you're not doing enough. But you have to look at your market and determine what it is you can do. People have all these dreams about what should be . . . and we got a lot of flack because people said we weren't doing enough black programming. But I didn't have a lot of money, and I had to make some hard decisions.

What was some of your original programming?

We had some hard-hitting news and information and some controversial issues. I have this great feeling that social programs tend to be designed more to keep jobs for middle-class people than to help the people the programs were designed to help. So we did a whole series on "poverty pimps" [laughs].

What were some of the other issues you addressed?

We had the school superintendent on for an indepth story. He defended himself very well. That was really great, I must say. We got a lot of calls asking for copies of

the tape. We did an analysis of the school budget and challenged the actual funding mechanisms of the system.
Because they had a lot of top-heavy people, a lot of Ph.D.'s
with no inner-city school experience. We challenged that.

So that was really localism, local news coverage, at its best.

Yes, you have to be local because that's the key that gets
you the viewers. On one of our programs, we actually went
to the mall and got people's point of view on key issues.
Then we did a whole thing on 9/11 where we found families in the Philadelphia area and went back every year and
did updates on how they were doing.

*We, the public, own the airwaves, but the government is
responsible for deciding who to lease space to on the dial. Can
you talk about the process of obtaining an FCC license?*

It took about eight years from the time that I applied
for Channel 48, the television station in Philadelphia, to
the time we went on the air. About six of those years
were spent fighting in court because I was challenged by
ten other groups who also wanted to buy it. They basically try to find fault with you. You know, you have to
have good standing because you're entrusted with this
public station. My competitors had somebody follow me.
They wanted to show that I was not a Little Miss Goody
Two Shoes. My sons were used against me. They said
they were dysfunctional, because they were going
through some problems. And they said that I lied about
my previous title. I had said on my application that

I signed checks at WWRL and that I was an assistant general manager there. Howard Saunders, who worked in sales and was the only other African American there with me at the time, testified on my behalf. But the station had thrown away all the boxes of paperwork from the old days that could have served as proof. Except one guy, Vince Sanders, who was general manager there, found an old box in the corner with stacks of checks, and there was my signature, big as day.

Even Egmont Sonderling, the previous owner of WWRL who had hired you, testified against you?
    Yes.

Why?
    You know, by then he had been immersed in the culture of America by the big guys. One of my competitors was Sinclair Broadcasting, and they were very persuasive. At one point, a representative from Sinclair even came to my office to offer me millions of dollars to step down. The check was already made out. My feeling is that by the time Sonderling came to Washington he had begun to relate more to white owners. I believe he testified against me because he began to assume some of the prejudices of America.

Why didn't you take the check?
    I knew that the station was going to be worth more than two or three million dollars. A lot more.

And, in the end, you were vindicated.

Yes. I was awarded the license by the first administrative judge early on in the process. But because my competitors continued to dispute the facts that were on my application, I had to defend myself all the way to the Supreme Court, where the judges agreed that I should be awarded the license. I got the final approval, I believe it was in 1990, and went on the air in August of 1992.

Most potential owners are out of money before they even get through the application process.

Yes, that's what they did back then. I knew a [Latina] owner who had a station in Florida. But when they finish with you, you're broke. I spent over $700,000.

But you were prepared?

No, I wasn't. I had to hock my radio stations halfway through the process. I sold WIGO in Atlanta, WEBB in Baltimore, and WBMS in Wilmington, North Carolina, around 1989. With so much debt, for me to try to run them and pay them off and the television station at the same time would have been impossible.

So you didn't want to give up those radio stations.

No, I didn't. But I had to. Those three little stations really could have been a foundation for a much larger network. But I just could not possibly keep them going.

If they hadn't contested your application, you would have been in a very different position.

Oh, I would have probably been a much larger broadcaster because I knew how to do it.

In 2004, you sold your Philadelphia television station WGTW, to the Trinity Broadcasting Network, which offers Christian programming, for $48 million. Why?

Well, age for one thing. And also the times have changed. Advertisers buy differently and the marketplace has broadened with satellite TV, cable having maximized itself, video, on-demand, you name it.

Did you have any potential African American buyers?

No. There are not many that I know of who have the money and who would want to operate a single UHF station, which has never been as strong of a signal as a VHF. Also with high definition and the expansion of media, it's impossible to pay that kind of money for just one station. Most African Americans don't have that kind of money for a single station, other than perhaps a Bob Johnson [former owner of Black Entertainment Television], who was getting out of the business, as opposed to coming in.

You used the capital from this sale to buy television stations in smaller markets, like Roanoke, Virginia, and Great Falls,

Montana. Why do you think black owners have had so little success in cable? It seems like we never had a chance.

No, we never did. And now it's over. As a matter of fact, radio is over, too. Now that Sirius and XM have merged with satellite, radio as a medium has probably lost 50 percent of its impact.

Recently GreenStone Media, the women's radio network that was founded by Jane Fonda, Gloria Steinem, and Robin Morgan in 2004, went out of business. You were an early investor in the company, along with high profile supporters such as Rosie O'Donnell. Why didn't it survive?

Overall, I'm not sure that the economics of how to make money were there. A lot of energy was put into the creative end of things but not as much on the financial aspects. If I were doing it, I would have made my focus be on the latter, as opposed to the former.

Will Radio One, the largest existing urban radio network in the country, be in trouble, too?

They'll survive because they've invested in satellite radio. And they also have TV One, so they've diversified. But they will never be the same. Even Clear Channel is not doing as well as they once were.

Who's to blame ultimately for the lack of minority media owners?

I think we're partly to blame because not a lot of people want to spend their lives digging in the dirt when they can walk away with five or ten million dollars and live well for the rest of their lives. I mean, how noble is the cause? Do you go for the greatness, or do you get your money and run? So, that to me is part of the problem. I think legislation is part of it. And I think the earlier denial of our entry into the medium because of race is part of it. But it's partly our fault because I don't think we have enough people who have the guts to stand in it and be competitive. It's big money, and there's a lot of risk. That's why I give Cathy Hughes all the respect in the world. She has fought to be a part of the system. And, yeah, she made money. And yeah, she's wealthy. But hell, what did it take to get there? Incredible risk and hard times and pain and suffering.

She literally lived at her radio station for a while, cooking on a hotplate.

Hey, I lived in mine, too. I was the janitor. I cleaned my toilets at night. That's what you do. Not many. When she would get depressed, she'd call me, and we would chat. And I would say hang on, you've got to fight. And she did.

Even after selling your radio stations, you still had to come up with $1.2 million for WGTW. How did you know the risk would pay off?

For me, it wasn't about a noble cause. I wanted to make money, and I liked doing what I did. I didn't make a lot of money with my radio stations, but it was enough to fight the battles I needed to fight, and pay off the bills. When I sold those AM stations, I think I netted about $250,000 for two. I used that little bit of money to buy the TV station. At the time, you could get into a TV station with $5 or 10 million, where today you would need $100 million. So it's how you leverage it. And then I was able to sell the TV station for bigger money. Survival became, for me, understanding how money works, where it comes from, and how it gets to where it goes.

You've said that winning in business is a "huge high" and that "money is the barometer that indicates you have done a job well." Some feel like you're not really down with the cause if you speak openly about a desire for money.

But see, we get so caught up in those imaginary boundaries. I like living well. I like eating well. I like traveling when I want to travel. I am pro-black because I realize you've got to eradicate the stigma, and I fight to do that. I will stand in a room of twenty thousand white males and dare to excel.

Do you think that's more important than joining movements?

I've never been a movement person. I would participate to the extent that I can lend a hand, but I don't attend meetings. You know, I've probably got twenty-nine memberships in the NAACP, lifetime memberships. But I will never march; never do any of that stuff. Because it takes away from my purpose, which is to open doors. I've opened doors at ABC for women, and I've actually put women on jobs because I know the general manager,

I know the owner. I would say, "You know, you need to do better." And they would say, "I can't find them." So I say "Oh." And I get on the phone and network. And then I'd pre-interview the people and send them. That was my thing: using the top to clear the way at the bottom.

How are consolidation and monopoly ownership changing the media landscape today?

You have to have multiple media outlets to survive. If I went to New York to pitch a national advertising buyer today, they're not just going to put together a budget for Philadelphia. They'll want to put together a budget for thirty stations. So it's a very difficult thing to start from zero. I sold the television station for $48 million. But to go from zero to $48 million takes a hell of a lot of work. And my sons didn't want to do it. So, you get what you can and get out before the bottom hits.

I read that even though you were poor growing up, your mother encouraged education and took you to the library in Harlem every week. Could you talk a little bit about your work in Africa? Does it correlate with your interest in the media?

Well, I tried to build a series of television stations in Ghana in the early 1990s. I went back and forth over there for twelve years. I had no phone and was way up in the hills of Ghana trying to build a hospital. I built a school there, too, and a library. I got the AKAs from Pittsburgh and all my sorority sisters to send me boxes of books and started a library. I started a school in Guyana, South

America. They made green uniforms, and we sent over barrels of crayons and books and stuff.

What happened with the television station in Ghana?

I did that for about three years. But there was so much distrust. The people who were running it didn't understand. I spent a lot of money. I even flew engineers in to do ground studies, but it just didn't work out. I was early. I was before my time. You know, it's not like you're following somebody. You're inventing as you go.

CHAPTER 7

BOOKER WADE

In 1980, when the FCC finally began to encourage greater diversity in broadcast ownership, Booker Wade, then thirty-three years old and a legal assistant to FCC Commissioner Tyrone Brown, decided to put in a bid for a piece of the pie, together with two attorney colleagues also at the commission, James Winston and Samuel Cooper. The lawyers announced their plan to purchase a low-power VHF/UHF television station in New York, the first of what they hoped would become a black-owned network that would eventually expand to include hundreds of urban stations nationwide.

They called the venture Community Television Network, and the timing for such a project, says Wade, was "beautiful." Well-positioned in terms of financing, the partners had secured a $60 million loan from Golden West Broadcasting, a media company owned by 1950s radio and film entertainer, Gene Autry. The signal for the station was to be sent from the Empire State Building, with a twenty-six-mile reach throughout New York City, as well as parts of New Jersey and Connecticut. Golden West would share air time with the network for seven years, while installing subscription boxes in suburban homes to amplify the signal. Despite the best-laid plans, however, the venture capsized. But Wade, now sixty, did not give up his dream of participating in media ownership.

Today, he is general manager of San Francisco's KMTP, one of only a handful of African American–controlled public television stations in the country. For years, his station was under assault from the cable owner, Comcast (and before that AT&T), which KMTP charged in February 2000 court documents with "an ongoing sustained pattern of rule violations," "willful manipulations," and "bad faith." Comcast, says Wade, dropped 70 percent of his station's subscribers without KMTP's knowledge in an effort to squeeze them out of business. "Their strategy," he said when we first spoke in 2005, "is to choke us to death so that we die."

Since then, however, KMTP and Comcast have made a kind of peace in the face of ever-changing technological and market-driven demands. The public television station has even managed to expand recently, setting up shop in spacious new offices just north of San Francisco, in Palo Alto, where I spoke to Wade again in the spring of 2007.

*   *   *

Let's start at the beginning. You worked at the FCC in the 1970s. What did you do there?

That was my first job out of law school. It actually sort of started with a wager with my law school classmates. You know, we were young and idealistic and out to change the world. I worked in licensing, in what was then called the Community Antenna Television Bureau. It was not even cable television yet in 1975. So basically when cable television systems added a new program, or a new service, they had to get approval with something called a certificate of compliance. My job was to review those applications. The job was very frustrating and bureaucratic. Really unimaginative. In fact, in retrospect, the job was essentially to protect broadcasters. In the early days of cable the commission's policy was to protect broadcasting, which was kind of like motherhood and apple pie, and cable was a threat to that. The commission did just about everything it could to hold it back for as long as it could. So I left in frustration after a couple of years and went into transportation.

Really?

Yes, I left media altogether, realizing that I needed to find another way. Then Jimmy Carter was elected president, and he appointed Tyrone Brown, an African American, to the commission. When I was there, Benjamin Hooks had become the first African American commissioner, and he laid the foundations for what was to come later. So I got in contact with Tyrone Brown and was fortunate enough to be appointed as one of his legal assistants.

So you were at the FCC at the same time as Jim Winston and Frank Washington, who are also in this book.

Absolutely. During the Carter administration, the commission came up with its now-famous policy on minority ownership. The percent now is obscenely low, but it was worse then.

Why did you decide to launch a television network?

Jim Winston, another former FCC attorney named Sam Cooper, and myself created the Community Television Network because we saw the opportunity for a nationwide black television network. We thought we could persuade the commission to create a new class of stations using the frequency space of low-powered television, which is substantially different from full-power television. So we had a plan for about ten stations that the network itself would own, and then we would encourage others to get affiliate stations in other cities.

How far did you get?

We got the licensing and funding to operate it. And we also were able to find the affiliates, do the engineering, and put together the infrastructure. We got that far. And that provided a national blueprint, which would have covered 85 percent of the African American population in the country. Once that was on file at the commission, to our astonishment, and I think to the world's astonishment, the network appeared to be much larger than what it was.

How so?

Well it was essentially a secondary service to the full-power stations. So, whereas full-power stations had mandatory carriage on cable television systems, we were not entitled to that. Full-power stations were also protected from interference. With low power, we were sort of squeezed into the middle of channels, but if we interfered, or if a full-power station needed our spectrum, we had to yield.

I see.

So we had lot of technical secondary status, and we thought, okay, this is not the regular networks, but we thought it would be sufficient to create a niche network at least as a starting point. And somewhere we thought we might be able to persuade the next commissioner to begin to give it some protection after we could demonstrate the value and the number of people served. We thought that the political, the economic, and the legal system would then give us greater protection because we were doing a community service. But let me back up a little bit. Once we filed our applications and we got relatively significant press, I think it sort of overwhelmed us and created an extraordinary magnet that was unjustified.

Because it wasn't as grand as it looked.

Right. But people saw it and said, "I can do this, too." And since the licensing process was basically one of open competition, anybody could try. And, therefore, people challenged us. We expected sixteen hundred applications in various parts of the country; the commission was overwhelmed with something like eighteen thousand applications for these low-powered stations. It was kind of like seats in a movie theater. There may have been hundreds of seats open, but people did not necessarily go to the unoccupied seats. They said, "You've got the best seat in the house. I want your seat."

So you had a lot of competition?

One of the biggest challenges to our network came from [the major retail company] Sears. They had what would now be called a private equity firm or venture capital firm that also went to work creating a network. They had planned to do programming that they called "Americana," a mix of movies, sitcoms, and variety. They simply overwhelmed us with resources.

And you think that's because of the press that came out of announcing your project?

It surely was in large part.

But Sears would not be a minority owner. Shouldn't that have given you an advantage?

Yes and no. Minority ownership then and now still has legal constraints on how far you can go with it until it becomes disadvantageous, as many people would phrase it, to nonminorities. Getting a license was on a "point," or comparative system. You get a point for being local. You get a point for being a new entry. And you get points for being minority ownership. But other people can also accumulate points. Also, the commission was simply not prepared for that kind of volume. There were only three people handling those applications. It took the commission fifteen years to address the backlog.

Fifteen years?

I would not be surprised if there were a few applications still sitting there unresolved today. The commission does a lot of things, and people often complain and write in, but I think the way it handled low-power requests was one of the most often-heard complaints. It was absolutely overwhelming for them.

Who wanted these low-power stations?

Every community group, every church, every small niche you could think of.

I heard about applications coming in from senior citizen groups, from nonprofits . . .

Yes, everybody.

How did you structure your investment financially?

We made a deal with the Gene Autry organization in Los Angeles, which also owned KTLA, the Los Angeles Dodgers, and some other media holdings. They agreed to provide funding for the core network in exchange for some of the air time. That created some serious debates

internally, but we sort of bit the bullet and made the compromise. They wanted a certain number of hours, and that
was a little uncomfortable. But we gave them a short-term
vision for say four or five years, and then the time would
revert back to us. In addition, we agreed to do a secondary
filing for additional stations in other markets to compensate for the loss. So on the whole it was a reasonably balanced deal that we thought we could live with.

How much did they put up?

It was a minimum guarantee of $65 million. Today it
would cost about $200 or $300 million to start something
like that. So I think people saw that and said, "Oh, my
God, this is a gold mine!" And then everybody came out.
We really underestimated the impact their interest would
have on the market. And we weren't even sure at this point
if concerned broadcasters may have been behind some of
the avalanches of competing applications.

Really?

Yeah. Broadcasters are interesting. I'm a broadcaster,
too, but I think they're too occupied by a fear of competition. I mean, for decades they've been totally insulated. In
the early years, the three networks were everything, and
they were so politically powerful that they didn't tolerate
competition. In the early years, broadcasting was extraordinarily profitable, with margins that most people would
think obscene. But they were so successful at controlling
everything that, even today, broadcasters are not yet comfortable in a competitive marketplace.

What kind of programming did you anticipate?

Our initial efforts would have been news and informational programming because that is the least expensive to launch. News wheels are the classic way that CNN launched.

That seems like a contradiction. Why do so many owners today say that producing news is too expensive?

Everything is expensive, but local news is the most expensive. Here at KMTP we do a nightly Pan-African news show, and we get more and better coverage from Zimbabwe or Kenya or South Africa than we can from Oakland, California.

Why?

Because the services that provide those international news stories are relatively inexpensive. Associated Press, the world's premier newsgathering organization, is so good, and so entrenched, and so comprehensive internationally, that getting a story from them produced in South Africa costs maybe $300. Whereas hiring a crew to go produce news in San Francisco would be prohibitive. It's kind of ironic.

So even if it does come from abroad, why do so many networks argue that they can't provide any substantive news whatsoever?

Well, let's pinpoint who's making those arguments. Do they mean, "I can't afford it because I was making a 40 percent margin, and now I'm down to a 22 percent?"

I would understand that. But the question is, "Is that 22 percent sufficient and adequate?" Of course it is. You could do news very well with that profit margin.

So saying they can't afford it is a ruse.

One of the broadcast industry's arguments is that in the old days, we had obscene profits, but we also subsidized the news and did a lot more things that were not necessarily bottom-line oriented. But now, they say, competition has forced us to become public companies and our shareholders won't allow us to invest over the long term. We need quarter-to-quarter profits, and that means better margins and less expenses. And news is a very expensive proposition. That's true. And that's because the nature of the industry has changed, and competition now comes from the Internet. I can respect that. But I still think you've got to look at it in context. You've dropped your margins, yes. But I'm sorry, single-digit margins are the norm in most industries, and the media needs to live with that. It doesn't mean you can't support news. It means you need to learn to support it in different ways.

So it's really just a resistance to change?

There has always been in media the point of view that something new on the horizon always threatens you. When television was first born, radio said, "Oh my God, we're dead." When FM was born, AM said, "Oh my God, we're dead." When cable was born, broadcast said, "Oh my God, we're dead." When satellite was born, cable said, "Oh my God, we're dead." And none of that has happened. What does happen is that each of those platforms reinvents itself in some way, and adjusts. AM radio stopped playing music and went to talk and information because FM had a better quality sound. Television and video can niche itself, too, rather than having networks that try to do everything: news, drama, and sports. CNN was the perfect example. And that's why some of the other networks thought, "Well, maybe I ought not to be in news because they're doing it."

When I first spoke to you and became interested in your story, it was in part because you mentioned that KMTP is the only channel in the country to have a nightly Pan-African newscast. With a thousand channels out there, how is this possible?

Probably not enough money in it. . . . Also the normal assumption might be that the African American audience is absolutely enthralled with it, but that's not the case. Our largest audience is among those who are not of African American descent.

Really.

Progressive, liberal whites in this market are our largest share of the audience. And one has to ask, "What does that mean?" Part of what it means is that for the African American audience, a lack of basic knowledge has somehow converted itself to a lack of interest. Take any news story, say the war in Iraq. Really it's kind of an update that you get. Because you come to that story with other knowledge about what's going on. But when you come to a story about [Zimbabwe President Robert] Mugabe and who is he, for example, you say, "Where is that? What's that all about?" You don't know enough to be interested. And you really can't digest it within the framework of the knowledge that you have.

How do we rectify that?

Part of our challenge is the classic public television challenge of educating not just the informed viewer about what happened in Zimbabwe today, but also providing background information to understand who the parties are and the issues. This kind of context is harder to put in a traditional two-minute news story. So we don't try. Most of our stories end up being three, four, or five times the length of a [network] news story because we have to lay out the history.

Can you talk a bit about the transition to digital television?

One of the nice things about our digital conversion is that since we will have more space, we'll be able to have an entire Pan-African news channel that will be able to provide a lot more in terms of mini-documentaries and major events.

You're going to have a separate channel?

Yes. The world of television as we know it is, technically, going to end in January of 2008. That's when analog television and all the channels that we're used to will have to be given back to the government, and we'll be granted new digital channels. Television is transitioning. That's a technical matter, but the net result is that broadcast stations will have more space for multiple channels. Space is not even the right word. We call it video streams. Digital is so efficient, in other words, that you can now send multichannels in the same spectrum space. It's called compression technology.

Can you explain that for the layperson?

Think of a freeway with multiple lanes. Now, you've got several lanes, and each channel is in each lane. But if I'm on a motorcycle, I don't really need all of that space. Digital technology allocates the space on a frame-by-frame basis, according to what you actually need. So since the motorcycle only needs a constricted amount of space, that allows for more information to come through. If a big rig comes through, the space widens again and takes the space from the motorcycle. But if nobody's in the space, the digital's got more room. So our new channel is 33, but really it will be 33.1, 33.2, 33.3, and so on.

That's fascinating.

Yes. So, literally, split frame by split frame, there is computer software that says, "You don't need that space," and the net result is that you can get multiple channels. How many is a product of how effective the digital compression technology is. Today, it can pump out five channels where there used to be one. In a few more years, we may be up to ten.

So the good news is that broadcasting is becoming a lot like wireless, and because of this, I think you'll see a lot more news. For example, here in San Francisco the Chinese population is 30 percent of the market, or more. In the future you will probably see at least one or two twenty-four-hour Chinese news channels.

So you're going to need a lot more programming.
And we're working on it. That's part of this expansion here.

I know about the battle KMTP had, first with AT&T and more recently with Comcast. You even had to close down at one point. How are you able to survive and even expand?
Pure persistence. The reality is you've got AT&T and the cable guys kicking your butt, and you just have to figure a way around it. It's not easy, but I think we've been able to do it because we're in a market that is persuasive about the need for diversity. That's a big starting point. We would not have been able to do this without the help of a lot of people. The first bow would be to ABC, CBS, and NBC in this market because they own the place where we put our antenna and transmitter. It's a community antenna, and the rent we pay is substantially lower than what we should be paying.

Why would the broadcasters help you?
Because this is public television, and I think they're enlightened enough to recognize that we're no real threat to them. It's a good community service. We offer Pan-African programming and Asian programming and we're serving a community that needs this. They still

send me a bill because I think for their accounting purposes, they have to.

But they know you're not going to pay it.

They know that. I mean, the digital transition requires new stuff at their tower and new antennas. . . . The total cost is something like $16 million, and each of the television stations has a surcharge that they have to pay in three or four months. We say, "Okay, we can't do that." So they say, "Alright, maybe we'll give you a ten- or fifteen-year deferment plan, or monthly payments." That has happened to us on many occasions.

How are you funded?

It's a public station so we don't have shareholders. A great majority of our support comes from small, independent retail merchants. We have a furniture store and a carpet company that contribute to our operating costs.

Are you member-supported?

Yes and no. Not in substantial numbers. By and large, 75 percent of our funding comes from small sponsors who pay on the average $1,000, $2,000, $3,000 per month to support us.

How many listeners do you have?

According to the last Nielsen survey the number of people who watch one or more of our programs, depending on the season and our schedule, obviously, is anywhere from three hundred thousand to four hundred fifty thousand per week.

And now you're on full time.

Right. We've been full-time for three or four years. That's always been a problem with cable and satellite because if you're in the cable system and you're only part time, the subscriber who's paying Comcast, or whoever, is going to think they're getting cheated. So we had to bite that bullet and go 24/7.

Where are things now with the Comcast battle?

When we started, our signal was distributed to less than 25 percent of the market. Today we're just under 80 percent.

But are you still fighting them in court?

Still battling. But basically it came down to a little arm-twisting from the FCC a few years ago. The FCC did not say that they had to carry us from everywhere, as we believed we were entitled to, but we had a mediation session and Comcast extended us to about 80 percent of the market. Since then, the commission has just been sitting on our complaint, not acting on it. That is their way of saying that's the deal.

When we spoke a few years ago, it seemed like you were really under pressure and Comcast wanted definitely to get rid of you.

Oh, they absolutely did.

I talked to Adam Clayton Powell III who helped you launch the station. He said that the cable company even resorted to tricks like taking off the children's programming at 5 p.m. and putting on a pornography channel.

And that goes back to prior to Comcast—

To AT&T?

And prior to that with Viacom. But the cable companies know that we're entitled to full carriage everywhere. They also know that we don't have the economic resources to wage an all-out legal war against them. So one of the sharpest points that the commission recognized was that we are serving several minority communities that present a growing market. And it doesn't stop there. The irony is that probably 80 percent of our members do not come from minority communities. The profile of our basic member who gives a contribution of $300–$500 is white and female, between the ages of thirty-five to fifty-five.

Why do you think they're watching?

Well, most of our programming is in English. Our linguistic programming is probably only three and a half hours a day, in German, Italian, and Chinese, and we used to do Vietnamese. We still do a little bit of Korean, but mostly Korean dramas with English subtitles, and those are directed to English-speaking audiences. But as a public station—and this is probably worth noting—we describe ourselves as an independent public station because we're not affiliated with PBS. I think there are only about five public stations in the country that are not PBS members.

There are five public stations in this market alone, and all of us used to be members of PBS. So doing *The NewsHour with Jim Lehrer* for the fifth time in one night is not what we're after. Our biggest program supplier, historically, has been Deutsche Welle, the German public television network consortium. We get news and lots of public affairs and lots of documentaries from Deutsche Welle. It's made up of four public television networks in a joint international venture, and together they provide programming in English, German, and Spanish. So you take their English, and historically an hour of their German programming, and it is top quality. It rivals the American networks in terms of news.

So you're offering a more international perspective.

And I think that's why so much of our audience is progressive, liberal, and mostly white. Our programming gives us a much more European view of diversity. In the lead up to the Iraq War, this was obvious. I mean people would say, "What? We didn't know that? We didn't hear that." And when all this debate was happening about France, suddenly we had their point of view and they were saying there's no evidence for this war. It was the opposite of what our administration was saying. So we got serious news analysis, and I think that really gives us a big boost in terms of credibility. George Bush is always in that news cycle and they have bureaus and reporters throughout the U.S. So we suddenly have this top-quality, international view of things, and we have an exclusive on it. It gave us a big boost.

Where are the other minority-operated public television stations in the country?

One is Channel 32, the Howard University station in Washington, DC. That board is minority controlled because it's run from the media department on campus, so it draws its budget from student fees and tuitions and endowments. There is one in New Orleans, a traditional PBS station that is licensed to the school board there. So it depends upon the election of school board members, whether or not that board will be African American–controlled, and it's gone back and forth. But, historically, public stations have been run by academic institutions. Ours is different in that we rely totally on our communities to support us.

Why does it matter that there are just a few minority-controlled public television stations?

Because of First Amendment constraints, the federal government cannot mandate a station to do certain kinds of programming, with some exceptions. So the commission has looked for a proxy for giving the best guarantee of producing diversity. Ownership has come to be that focus. If you look historically, you'll find that media that is owned and controlled by minorities is more likely to produce diversity in programming than any other mechanism. And that's understandable. If I happen to be Vietnamese, I probably have some interest in serving that community. Because I know it. I feel it and sense it. Much of media, whether it's film or news or documentary, is storytelling, and I tell stories with my family, my friends, and my community. I can tell others, but I'm also

likely to tell those. Someone without those experiences is
not as likely to do this.

Why are you independent public television?

Public generally means PBS to most folks, but that's not
our definition or our mission. We are public because regulatory constraints force us to be. This was the only eco-
nomically available full-power station. In other words, the
acquisition of the station didn't cost us anything; it was
given to us by regulatory directive. If we had to purchase a
station in this market it would cost $40–$50 million,
which would have been outside of our capacity. So we had
to take what was offered, which was public television.
Twice in my career I've made efforts to start national black
networks. One was Community Television Network,
which I told you about. And the other was something we
called the Corporation for African American Television,
which mimicked the Corporation for Public Television.

Oh, I heard a little about that.

In 1990, the commission had reserved about 166 channels for public television in major markets such as Cleveland, Memphis, New Orleans, and Atlanta. They were
sitting idle and had been sitting idle for twenty years. So I
approached the Corporation for Public Broadcasting,
which gets money from Congress to develop public stations, and asked them to provide funding to activate these
dormant stations. They were totally uninterested. They
just simply did not want to fractionalize the PBS audience.

They said, essentially, that PBS provides sufficient diversity for minorities. So clearly, AT&T and Comcast and cable folks don't want this, and clearly the CPB doesn't want it, but clearly our viewers want it.

And that's why you have hung on for so long.

I love it. It's a mission. For a while, I got out and practiced law, and fortunately I was able to earn a good amount of money doing that. It gave me the freedom I need to do this without having to worry.

CHAPTER 8

MELODY SPANN-COOPER

When WVON-AM (then known as "Voice of the Negro") first went on the air in 1963, it was housed in a seventy-eight-hundred-square-foot station on the edge of Lake Michigan. Later, the station that had been owned by Jewish-Polish immigrants Leonard and Phil Chess of Chess Records was purchased by popular African American deejays Pervis Spann and Wesley South. It became an institution in the city of Chicago with profound political and social power among its loyal audience. Today, the station and its forty employees are expanding.

Melody Spann-Cooper, forty-two, the daughter of Pervis Spann, became general manager of the station in 1994, and in 2001, took over as the sole owner. In 2007, she relocated into a significantly more lavish seventeen-thousand-square-foot headquarters—parts of which will be used as both a community resource center and a museum honoring local radio legends. The new facilities have state-of-the-art studios, and for the first time in the station's history, a kitchen. This has all been possible because of an unprecedented partnership that Spann-Cooper sealed with radio conglomerate Clear Channel in 2006. It is an agreement that makes some of her supporters suspicious. Admittedly, says Spann-Cooper, it was a risky move that made her nervous. But she argues, convincingly, that the deal was the key to her station's survival and growth.

During my visit, I also had an opportunity to speak with Pervis Spann, seventy-five, who still visits from time to time and maintains a small office. Although many of those interviewed in this book believe that the FCC did finally provide limited opportunities for minority ownership beginning in the 1970s, Spann's recollection of the agency was not so positive. "The FCC was always prejudiced," he said. "I don't recall them being interested in selling to black folks at any time." He does remember, however, being invited to a small gathering hosted by President Carter, a meeting that was set up in the late 1970s to encourage minority ownership, which Spann attended.

Over the years, Spann says that he filed petitions for ownership for a number of radio stations. "I went to Washington a lot of times," he says. He was eventually granted licenses in Memphis (James Brown was an investor), Atlanta, and Zeeland, Michigan, on the other side of Lake Michigan. "I went over there and paid the man whatever, $150 or $200 for the frequency," he recalls, "and tried to reach Chicago." When asked what made him think that he could acquire radio stations, Pervis Spann said this: "I couldn't come up with a reason why I shouldn't. It was open, so we went for it."

*   *   *

WVON has such an amazing history. Can you talk about how your father, Pervis Spann, also known as "The Blues Man," bought the station?

My dad was a disc jockey who was part of the original WVON that went on the air in 1963. Wesley South, who became his partner, also had a very popular talk show called "Hotline." As a matter of fact, the show was so popular that WVON was often the number-one station in the market with only one thousand watts. When [slain civil rights activist] Medgar Evers died, there were so many calls coming into the station that it shut down the whole phone system on the west side for weeks. Wesley South knew all the politicians. He interviewed Malcolm X, Robert F. Kennedy, you name them. They would come in for his talk show that was on just before my dad's midnight blues show. In the daytime, my dad had another business. He owned nightclubs. He was the one who actually crowned Aretha Franklin the "Queen of Soul." He booked The Jackson Five, Sam Cook, Aretha Franklin, and others at the Regal Theater. So that's where he made his money. Radio was just a side bar.

How did he end up owning the station?

In the 1970s, new owners bought the station. And since dad and them were getting older—I guess maybe in their forties—the new owners came in and fired everybody. They just blew out the entire place. They wanted new and fresh. So my dad went to Wesley South and said, "I got the money. You got the political connections. Let's get our own radio station." They moved [the call letters] WVON and went into business.

But the station's signal was shared.

Yes. Until recently, we were the only radio frequency in the country that shared a signal. That happened because there was another station that had filed with the FCC around the same time that my dad applied, and it was Polish owned. My dad thought that since they had already given a station in the market to an African American, he worried that if they competed, the Polish people would win. So they decided to share the frequency.

You've said that your father and Wesley South were like "oil and water."

Wesley knew politics and political people. He could go and deal with the lawyers. He had the right acumen. He was intelligent, and he had a great name. My dad came from the South and didn't have the formidable education that you would think he would have to do all the things that he's done. But dad was the money man. He could pay the lawyers. He had amassed a nice little war chest. They weren't running buddies, but it was a great partnership.

Today you are one of the few surviving black media owners in the country. How did you do it?

I don't look at radio in a traditional sense. My vision goes beyond WVON as just radio. My mission is more community based. WVON is an institution in the city of Chicago. It's like Wrigley Field: Chicago embraces it. And people are always willing to help and make sure that we're okay. I got on the air when we needed some money, and I'm about to do it again.

I interviewed a former radio owner in Syracuse, New York, who ultimately lost his station a few years ago. One of the things he says is that he didn't know how to ask for financial help from the black community he served.

Because he was trying to be traditional radio, but there's nothing traditional about us. How can I compete with Clear Channel? I'm in the heart of one of the great middle-class black communities in the country, Chatham. I'm in the building that was the former headquarters of Soft Sheen products. The [former Soft Sheen] owner, Mr. Gardner, owned seven buildings here. Seaway, a famous black-owned bank, is down the street. George Johnson, who owned Ultra Sheen, one of the largest black-owned hair care manufacturers, was also here. The Collins Brothers [beverage retailers], who few people talk about, owned these corners. So this has always been a bevy for African American businesses. And now you have another generation coming to occupy this space in an era where you see so many people leaving black communities and going elsewhere to do business.

Chicago is still very much segregated.

Chicago is one of the most segregated cities in the country. From the time you leave 35th Street all the way until you pass the city borders, there's nothing but African Americans. You're not going to find an integration of whites or Hispanics. It's just how we flow.

Your listeners are incredibly powerful here, and business owners and politicians know it. Are they afraid of your power?

I don't want to call it afraid. I want to say aware. But I don't pull that card. You've got to do something very, very bad for me to pull it. We're here to keep the community informed of what is going on. My goal is to make my people think and to make rational decisions based on the truth that I am putting before them. You know I am amazed by this whole debate with [Illinois senator and presidential candidate] Barack Obama. It would be very easy for me to get on the air and say, "Hey. Barack's my man." But I want African Americans to understand that they have choices.

When you need help, the community opens its wallet.

I asked for funds a couple of years ago, and it helped us so much that we were able to then turn that money over to a 501(c)(3). That's how I'm building this museum; my listeners will build it. And that funding helps with programming that I can't get advertiser support for. For example, I celebrate pre-Kwanzaa. I celebrate Juneteenth. But I can't go to Coca Cola and say, "Celebrate Juneteenth." They'll say, what the hell is Juneteenth?

All of the radio station owners I've spoken to say that racism, or racial ignorance, among advertisers is still a huge impediment.

That is my fight every day. And they don't do that when it comes to white folks. They buy Don Imus, Howard Stern, and everyone else. But I go to Pepsi and say, "Hey, I got pre-Kwanzaa." They say, "What's pre-Kwanzaa? Is Jay-Z going to be there?" You understand what I'm saying? It's a tough fight. But these listeners are not going to let the station go down. They are just not going to let it go down.

How does someone like [popular celebrity deejay] Tom Joyner manage to get so much advertiser support?

Tom Joyner has five million listeners. They don't give a damn if he sells widgets. With five million they can justify it. Tom Joyner is an awesome example of somebody who's gone outside the box and is doing great things for his community. I love him for that. I think it's awesome. But when you're sitting on 87th Street, and you've got maybe two hundred thousand listeners, my numbers look quite a bit different.

In 2006, you entered into a Local Marketing Agreement, or LMA as it is known in the industry, with Clear Channel. What does that mean?

It's a lease management agreement, like renting an apartment. It says I am going to take your signal and run my programming off of it. I'm going to run the radio station, but you own it. They own the signal.

Does Clear Channel own the call letters?

Well, we did that on a swap. I moved my call letters, WVON, over to their signal, 1690 AM. It was an interesting deal. I'm surprised it didn't get more attention. This is a company that's probably the largest radio conglomerate in the world. They sent a new manager into this marketplace, [regional vice president] Earl Jones, to turn their stations around and make them make them more profitable. They were playing oldies music on an AM dial. But times have changed. So Earl had to do something with the signal. One of his choices was to compete with me and do a black talk station.

Did you know Clear Channel was thinking about competing with you at the time?

Yes. Earl Jones called and told me. Everybody was trying to figure out, "How is this girl staying in business?" So he called and said, "First of all, I'm new in town, and people are telling me I need to meet you. And second, I got this station over here, and I'm trying to figure out what to do with it. And one of the things that is being considered is a black talk station, but I don't want to compete with you."

Was he the only one there who thought that would be a bad move?

Let's say this: He was conscious enough to understand that this was a black-owned station and that Clear Channel did not need to come in here and be the big piranha and run us out of business. Thank God we sat down and talked. He initially said, "Why don't you run this station and get enveloped in the Clear Channel family, and let's create a new paradigm in ownership?"

What does that mean?

I have a lot of fear there. When I get combined with Clear Channel, do I still have the freedom to do what I want to do with my station? Will it still be authentic? Will the message get diluted because I'm white owned? Do I become a BET? I don't want to do that. Bob Johnson sold BET, and I can't, quite frankly, tell much of a difference between what BET was doing when he owned it and what it's doing now. But people's perceptions are that it changed and that it's watered down. With a black talk format, I can imagine it being watered down under a Clear Channel.

So how did you get to the LMA agreement?

When Earl Jones told me that somebody made him an offer to lease the station, I said, "Well, why don't you just lease it to me?" It wasn't a bad proposition. They still get paid. But it was contingent on me being able to line up my [financial] ducks like anybody else. They didn't do me any favors, or offer any special breaks. It was not an affirmative action plan.

Did it help that Earl Jones is African American?

You know, let me just say this: there was an African American gentleman in that position before him who didn't offer me this opportunity. If Earl Jones hadn't been an "out-of-the-box" thinker who had a consciousness for African American business, it would not have happened. He knew he could hurt me. He also knew he could help me. And he knew it wouldn't hurt Clear Channel one way or the other to help me. It could do nothing but make Clear Channel look good. I think it was a major coup for both of us. Because Clear Channel had some PR problems in this market, and when they came out with this deal, people said, "Wow."

You also negotiated an option to buy the station. How did that come about?

One night I started thinking, "Okay, this deal is for five years. Now if I understand business people, if I'm making money in five years, they're going to come back and take it and say, 'Go back to your little 1450 AM, girl.'" So I called Earl and said, "Earl. You know I can't do this deal without at least an opportunity to buy it out." He said, "Melody, we don't sell radio stations off, especially not in a market like Chicago." I said, "Earl. In a market like Chicago, this little 1690 AM station, what is this to Clear Channel? I didn't ask for one of your FM signals. I didn't ask for one of your main properties. I'm asking for this little AM signal that can't even compete with you most days. Just ask them what will it cost for me to buy the station."

How long did it take to get an answer?

You know, I didn't hear back from Earl for like three weeks. When he came back, he said they agreed to sell you the station.

So you get what you ask for.

And you got to make it make sense for them. You can't go asking for the affirmative action plan.

How does this deal help you to grow?

The frequency that I was on before was the only radio frequency in the country that shared a signal. I actually signed off at one o'clock in the afternoon, and another station came on. People were amazed that I was doing the kind of inventory I was doing, going off the air at one o'clock. It showed that I had potential. Before, my signal was one thousand watts and probably went to 130 miles on a good day in a car. Now, my signal is ten thousand watts, and it will take you all the way to Minnesota. That's important because there are now as many African Americans living in the suburbs as there are in the city, but I couldn't reach them on my former signal. So this was not only a great opportunity for WVON, it was a decision I had to make because of the changing demographics of Chicago.

Even before the deal, you were already under construction with this new building, which you financed through a municipal tax credit of $1 million. How were you able to get that?

Everything in Chicago is political. This particular area is run by a John Sloger, who's an alderman, and his son was an alderman. When I decided to buy the building, John was the first person I called. I said, "I'm thinking about buying a building, and I'm going to need some help." He said, "Come to my office." I went to his office on a Monday night, and he had a gentleman from the Department of Planning there. He said, whatever you need. So they gave me a million dollars, and that's what I paid for the building. But then I also did $4 million worth of renovation. Part of the money from the city comes from the green garden on the rooftop, which is Mayor Daley's pet project. Every big project in the city now that gets any funding has to do a green garden for energy efficiency.

As you grow and expand, some of your older listeners are worried that the station is moving away from its programming roots. You hired CNN commentator Roland Martin, whose point of view is often different from the old guard here.

I got a lot of new voices on. It's like Moses and Joshua in the Bible. Moses was an old guy, and Joshua was the young guy coming up. I think Roland is a burst of energy. I think he's dynamic. He's a strong, confident black man who hasn't been broken. And because he never marched, he doesn't understand that experience and doesn't have any old contextual stuff to bring to it. He's just wild and free. He wasn't even born yet in 1968. And we have Santita Jackson on, she brings another flavor. As Reverend Jesse Jackson's eldest daughter, she sees through the eyes of a father who has given his life to the advancement of black folks. She sees a community that's not the same and a lot of it is because of her dad's contributions. He will never get credit for that, though, because we don't know what to do with a civil rights leader who gets to be sixty-five. And then you got [afternoon talk show host] Reverend Al Sharpton, and of course Al brings it every day. You've got [former city council member and alderman] Cliff Kelley. He's strong on politics, he's old-school, and he's intelligent beyond his audience, which to me sometimes is a downside because he talks over their heads. On foreign policy he knows everything there is to know. He knows too damn much. Then I've got some young guys who come on in the evening. They have the potential to be in the top ten in Chicago radio. They are just stupid and funny, and white people like them, too. So I'm excited about my format. And I'm starting to see some movement in my numbers. If I can just get through this year, I'm going to be okay. This is the hardest thing I've ever done. I mean, man! These bills!

As your mentor, Radio One owner Cathy Hughes put it, you have to either "grow or die."

Right, that's right. But let me be perfectly honest with you: a lot of us "Ma and Pa" owners stay bogged down in a mentality where we only see that payroll is today. I can't sit here and tell you I can go on vacation. Because payroll is today, and I'm trying to find $25,000 as I sit here with you. Does that mean Melody is going out of business? Uh uh. It just means this is how my business is going with all of my growth. For many of us, we stay on a perpetual treadmill of survival. And this is not just about media owners. This is black businesses.

Yes.

Even Bob Johnson . . . you can't tell me that he wasn't on a perpetual treadmill running BET. So when he sold, I was like, "My man. Free at last." I was the lone voice maybe, but I understood. You get tired. I'm forty-two okay? I got about eight more good years of this. At fifty, I'm cashing out. See ya. Because this stuff is that hard. It's rewarding, but it's hard.

Do you think you'll be able to sell WVON to a black owner?

Hope so. Want to. But we need a lot of internal work. And we need to admit that we don't know. A lot of people couldn't understand it when there was a [FCC minority ownership] tax incentive. Even with the special incentives, we don't get it. *We do not get it.* And it's something that we don't want to admit. When the tax incentive was in place, how many of us took advantage of it? We want to put on these suits and go into these meetings and nod our heads like we get it, and pontificate at the table, but we go home, and nothing changes. We have to be honest. We've got to ask for help. This stuff that I've done here, I can't tell you how this all came together. I know God has been good to me. I do know that. But I also know my banker, and my banker knows me. My banker has done every deal I've ever done in business. She understands my flow. If you don't know the person that you're giving your resume to, to walk it upstairs, chances are you're not going to get that job. We've got to become smarter. Damn what industry we're in! It could be radio, it could be widgets, or it could be finance. Do we understand the business side of being in business?

To grow you've had to take on a lot of debt, and that's scary for people.

It's debt, but I wouldn't consider it bad debt. This is a time when they're spending hundreds of millions of dollars for radio stations. And you know what? At the end of the day, we're just moving paper.

True.

Clear Channel buys stations for $300 million. Do you think they're actually writing a check? No. They're moving paper. They're paying the bill, moving the paper. So what am I supposed to do? Say no? You got to jump. You got to pray, hold your breath, and jump.

How did you learn all of this?

I've been at this station since I was fourteen. I've had an opportunity to work in every department here. There are fundamentals, but my greatest knowledge came from hard knocks: somebody knocking on the door when the station is in receivership and I'm the receiver. The IRS man saying I need $33,000 on Monday. Hard knocks. I didn't know what the Illinois Department of Unemployment Security was. Or that we were thousands of dollars in debt with them.

How did you become owner of the station?

Mr. South and my dad fought for many, many years. That's how I ended up in charge. The courts finally got tired of it. The judge could have ordered the station to be sold if we didn't settle, because our case had been there five years. So they both agreed that I was honest, I had come up in the station, and I had shown that I could run the business. They felt comfortable in that. When the judge got tired of us, she first gave Daddy an opportunity to buy out the minority shareholders because minority shareholders represented the swing vote for either one of them. But my dad does not handle business right. He should probably be one of the richest men in Chicago had he handled his business correctly. So then the judge gave Wesley South an opportunity to do it, and he didn't come up with the money either. So the judge was getting tired, and she looked at me, and she said, "Why don't you all just sell the station to Melody?"

You had the money.

I got a way to get the money! All I needed to do was buy the minority shares out.

Was it the same judge the whole five years?

Well, actually one judge retired on us. Then this one came on and she was like, "Oh, no! Not five years. This has got to go." She called us to court on a Saturday and said we were not leaving until it was settled.

Why do you say your dad doesn't handle business correctly?

Here in Chicago, they offered my dad the number-one FM station, which is now WGCI. I think they offered it to him for $28,000. It's now worth $200 to $300 million. You know, the beautiful thing about [Inner City Broadcasting cofounder] Percy Sutton is that they offered him WBLS in New York, and he paid little, or nothing, for it. Today, it's one of the strongest FM signals in the country in the largest market in the country. And there is an African American man that owns this FM powerhouse. Dad didn't have that foresight. His vision did not take him there. This FM band sat there idle and was there for the picking. But to them, it probably looked like Sirius Radio looks now or these satellite radio stations. It was foreign. All they ever knew was AM radio.

Your father says that as a child you always believed you could do anything you wanted.

And guess where I got that from?

He's seventy-five now. How does he feel about no longer being on the air?

I'm thinking about asking him to spin some music at night for a couple of hours. He's getting up in age, though, and his mind is not what it was. I don't really want him out at night.

Does he ever see Wesley South?

Yes! He comes by. It's amazing because now I watch them walk around together, and sometimes they sit down and talk. Wesley is ninety-four, and Daddy is seventy-five. It's amazing for them to see that the station is still carrying on. They should be proud.

CHAPTER 9

CHAUNCEY WENDELL BAILEY, JR., AND LEONARD D. STEPHENS

Slain journalist Chauncey Bailey (1949–2007) was a crusading reporter who lost his life in August of 2007 while working on a story that would have exposed the shady business and criminal practices at Your Black Muslim Bakery in Oakland, California. Gunned down in broad daylight by a killer who was not much older than his own thirteen-year-old son, Bailey is remembered for his dedication to the local black Bay Area community.

But what is not as well-known is the fact that Bailey did not believe journalism was the sole terrain of the elite. He believed in community access to media. And he believed in cable television. And so, armed with letters of recommendation from the Oakland mayor and from members of the city council, he spent many months meeting with Comcast executives and with potential investors, arguing for the importance of local African American programming in Oakland.

The result of this work was OUR TV, or "Opportunities in Urban Renaissance," a small leased-access cable channel that Bailey launched together with his partner and financier, Leonard Stephens, forty-six, in December of 2004. Channel 78, which is on from 6 p.m. to midnight seven days a week, reaches more than one hundred fifty thousand homes in the predominantly black areas of Oakland, Piedmont, and Emeryville, and it's growing.

The predecessor to OUR TV was Soul Beat TV, launched in 1978 by famed deejay Chuck Johnson, who some say created the original business model that would inspire Bob Johnson's Black Entertainment Television (BET) two years later. Supporters of Chuck Johnson (no relation to Bob) say that his was the first African American music video network in the country; it was also the channel that launched the breakout careers of Oakland rap artists Digital Underground, MC Hammer and Too Short.

Unlike Bob Johnson, however, who partnered with John Malone's Tele-Communications Inc. (TCI is now known as Liberty Media) to create BET, Chuck Johnson was determined to keep Soul Beat TV black owned, local, and independent. Using a model that was uncommon for his time, he was able to lease a slot on the local cable system, then operated by AT&T. In 1997, when the IRS shut Soul Beat down because of $37,000 in unpaid taxes, Johnson appealed to his viewers for support and managed to muster up $40,000 within a week. Even teenagers came "with mason jars filled with pennies," according to the Soul Beat

Web site. Johnson's low-budget, volunteer operation was able to stay on the air largely because it provided a much-needed public service to the community. It helped to locate missing children who would not have received coverage on mainstream news outlets, and it played a major role in organizing local health care screenings for diabetes and cancer.

When Comcast took over the area's cable system in 2003, however, the slot that Soul Beat had occupied, Channel 49, was given to TV One, the new African American–oriented network launched by Radio One and Comcast in 2004.

Still, Johnson kept his station going for a few more months, via a low-frequency radio station and Internet webcast. "Even while his health was declining, and he was forced to use a wheelchair," says former Soul Beat news director Chauncey Bailey, "he never gave up." Johnson, who was the first black general manager of the Los Angeles radio station that would later become K-ACE in 1962, and the first black owner of a California FM radio station in 1964, died of cancer in July of 2004.

As a primary heir to the Soul Beat legacy, Bailey banded together with Leonard Stephens to become cofounders of OUR TV, which launched in December of 2004. Last spring, just a few months before Baily's tragic murder, I spoke with Bailey and Stephens for more than two hours in the modest reception area of their East Oakland studio.

*   *   *

It is not possible to talk about OUR TV without first talking about Soul Beat TV, its predecessor. Chauncey, what was your role at Soul Beat?

Chauncey Bailey: I was news director for eight years and was on camera with a daily news show. At the time, I also worked as a reporter for the *Oakland Tribune*, so I could pull up stories that would never get into the paper—stories about black farmers or Louis Farrakhan—and use them at Soul Beat. The channel was very rudimentary, very Third World in terms of production. We didn't have a teleprompter. And there were technical problems. We're much better packaged now.

What happened after it was taken off the air?

CB: Soul Beat was put up for sale for $3 million, but investors didn't think it was worth that amount. It probably wasn't. We were basically trying to buy the legacy, which was both good and bad. Eventually, I realized that we had to start from the ground up.

Leonard Stephens: Chauncey also helped start KBLC, a black station here, which was initially on for twenty-four hours. They had some, I want to say, financial problems. They didn't expect some of the expenses that were required for a station to run twenty-four hours. Kelvin Lewis, who founded it, wanted to pull out of his prime time slot because he needed to cut back on his expenses. So that opened up a time for OUR TV and for another channel, VJ TV, which plays music videos all day, in the same format as Soul Beat. Allowing music to play continuously in a two-hour loop is very low maintenance. So it's a very smart operation they have over there at VJ TV. But OUR TV has input from churches and community programs. We cover sports at the high school. We're constantly in the community. That's what separates us from TV One, VJ TV, and KBLC.

CB: I think you can beat the big guys if you're community based. Comcast also needs us because they need relevant black programming. We're an asset to them.

LS: Initially, what Comcast was trying to do was get all three of us on one channel.

CB: They wanted to ghettoize us on one channel.

LS: Which is what they've done. Now we're all on Channel 78. They told us that they were doing some sort of fiber optic expansion and that in a year or so there would be more channels available. But we also have programs playing on Channel 26 and 27. So basically, with the three local channels, we have what we call a network, not a station. We're on Channel 29 in San Francisco, as well. And by the end of the year, we'll have more time. We have a couple of programs that are playing in Pittsburgh, and I have one program that's playing on twenty different channels.

CB: In five hundred thousand homes.

LS: Right. All of our programs go out to two hundred seventy-five thousand homes in Richmond, Berkeley, and Oakland. And we also have several programs that play on all three grids, which go out to over half a million homes. We have programs that are playing in Richmond, Berkeley, El Cerrito, El Sobrante, San Pablo, Oakland, Piedmont, Emeryville, Alameda, San Leandro, San Lorenzo,

Hayward, Union City, Newark, and Fremont. Okay, so that's over a half million homes in the greater Northern East Bay. But our base channel, which is on from 6 p.m. to midnight, seven days a week, reaches over one hundred fifty thousand homes. That's Oakland, Piedmont, and Emeryville: the Oakland Grid.

So Leonard, you're not originally from the media world. What's your day job?

LS: My other business, which I've done for twenty years, is quality assurance consulting for manufacturing companies like Ashland Chemicals, Squibb, and Corning. I write procedures, create records, facilitate meetings, audit, and prepare companies for third-party registrations. I make recommendations, and if the companies decide to implement them, I train them and monitor them. My company is called Audit Pro. I started it when I left IBM, where I worked for eight years.

How did you get involved with OUR TV?

LS: I'm an avid golf fan, so it started because I wanted to get this video on TV called "Golf Aerobics" that helps to develop muscle memory. My golf instructor was a man named Bob Johnson [no relation to the founder of BET] who grew up at a time when blacks weren't allowed to play on the golf course. He started as a caddy, and when he told me his story, I was really moved by it. He became a mentor and role model for me. So when I heard that Chauncey was having a meeting for programmers—I guess OUR TV was just a gleam in his eye at that time—I wanted to get Bob's program on television. Chauncey had meetings every Friday, actually. I kept going, and I kept volunteering because I thought, "If I can do programming, then Bob's program is going to be on TV. So four or five meetings down the road . . ."

CB: I had held other meetings with potential investors before, but it turned out that the other people were from TV One. I found out about that later.

LS: When I was trying to be a programmer, Chauncey ignored me for like three weeks. I kept saying, "I'll do it, I'll do it." But for some reason he passed me over. Then finally he gave me a shot. So after about the fifth meeting we all sat around the table. At that time, there were about twelve or fifteen of us.

CB: The group had dwindled.

LS: Right. And we had to decide who would be a leader. Everyone said I should do it. I've never been a back-seat person. When I do my consulting, I'm the driver. So I came in and put together flow charts and graphs . . . and ever since that day, I've taken this on as a way of life. It's not necessarily a job.

CB: You called it a ministry.

LS: It is my ministry. I feel a spiritual tie of giving back to the community, and I also feel that I'm spiritually tied to Chuck Johnson.

OUR TV first went on the air December 18, 2004. How did you negotiate carriage with Comcast, which was also launching TV One at the time?

LS: Chauncey and I had met with [Comcast executive] Bill Dodge and a gentleman from sales in Richmond, California. We outlined what we wanted to do, why we needed African American programming, and why it was important to the community. We also had letters of recommendation from the mayor and from city council members.

CB: In the beginning, I think they saw us as competitors. But we had to convince them that we were separate fingers on the same hand and that we were complementing TV One. We also showed them that there were some rumblings in the community. People were still upset that Soul Beat was gone and they were looking for a local replacement. TV One didn't fill the void. We enjoy TV One, and we embrace it, but I don't think we need to watch [classic 1970s sitcom] *Good Times* eight times a day. We need diversity. And we need local programming.

Why?

CB: Because without it local issues and local talent often get overlooked. People know they can't get on BET or VH1, but they can come in here and make a video and get on our channel. We have a show called *The Beat Is Going On* that allows young people from the area to perform spoken word and hip hop, and gives them a creative outlet. Oakland has a history of having a strong independent, underground music industry and culture.

LS: *The Beat Is Going On* is like a poor man's Apollo Theater. The kids are able to come here, and we shoot a video for them. They get exposure. We take videos and dance routines from local kids, try to keep them off the streets, give them something positive to do. They come in, and they work hard. We've had at least one hundred rappers on from Monterey to Sacramento. We also have programs that come from churches and community organizations. We have Joe Lewis and his cultural show and David Scott with *Christian Comedy*. We have Suzanne Mason with *Up Close and Personal* and Miss Punkin's *Showdown Throwdown*. We're smack dab in the middle of the blackest zip code in Oakland: 94605. And we're just happy to have an opportunity to be the soundboard for the community.

How is your relationship with Comcast?

LS: From a business standpoint, we need them. They allowed us a platform in order to launch, and they do give us certain perks.

What kind of perks?

LS: They've been lenient on some things like deadlines, and they've allowed us to expand in some areas on a trial basis before we actually start leasing time. One of the problems that KBLC had was that they tried to start off with twenty-four hours. You have to let it grow gradually. Because if you've got all this time and no programming. . . . What did you say ESPN started off with, Chauncey?

CB: ESPN started off with half an hour. And MTV started off with half an hour.

What's your business model? How do you generate revenue?

LS: Our mission was to be affordable and accessible. My colleague Ansaro Muhammad had some ideas. And I had an idea called Info-vision, which is a cooperative advertisement. For $79.99, the small advertiser can have their message on a jpeg, with a picture of their business, and it can be on television seven days a week, more than 120 times. When we've got eighty people paying $79.99, they're helping one another. It's like a video yellow pages.

So it's like the TV Guide channel, where programs scroll down at the bottom of the screen and Joan Rivers or somebody is at the top?

LS: Right. In the big window, we have a program. And down below we have businesses that will sit for ten to twelve seconds, and then the next business will come up. This way we can take cooperative small dollars for a community bulletin board, and recirculate our dollars by utilizing one another's services. Even the State of California contacted us to advertise for their low-cost automobile insurance.

CB: Most of our advertisers are local black-owned car dealerships, clothing stores, boutiques, hair salons. It's been difficult because a lot of African American businesses don't have advertising as part of their psyche. We're trying to get folks out of the culture of flyers and into putting their message on television.

LS: I'm laughing because our business partner here, Chauncey, is really good with community relations, and he brings a lot of business to us. But if he had his way, bless his heart, he would just open up the network to anybody that wanted to use it.

CB: We wouldn't make money.

LS: We wouldn't be able to survive. [Laughs] So with the rappers, we review what they want, and if they have a budget for it, we produce the video. But there have been times where they didn't have a budget, and we had to eat the costs. That's happened more times than I'd like to remember.

Essentially, you're functioning as a production company, too.

LS: We're functioning as a production company and a broadcasting network.

And you have community-based news and informational programs.

LS: Yes, we're not charging anybody for that. That's something that we want to sponsor so that your voice can be heard.

What news and informational coverage do you offer?

LS: We covered the [2006 Oakland mayoral campaign] of Ron Dellums quite vividly. We also had a show hosted by Ed Dillard, who is president of the Oakland Black Board of Trade and Commerce. He had a show on called *Bay Area Business Today.*

How was your coverage of the Dellums campaign different from that of mainstream news outlets?

LS: The mainstream would just basically give you sound bites. We showed his entire speech. If Comcast tried to do what we do here in Oakland, they would not be successful. They don't have the reach that Chauncey has. Chauncey was at the *Oakland Tribune* for twelve years, and he was the only African American news writer there at that time. He was on-camera at Soul Beat for eight years. He represents the community, and he was instrumental in getting the whole concept started. All I did was come along to polish it and manage it.

CB: Soul Beat was definitely a political power broker in the black community. We talked about issues; we had politicians on. So we inherited that influence. We do a daily newsmagazine that addresses high crime areas, and we have a show called *Express Yourself* where we take our cameras out to a busy intersection, and give people thirty seconds to vent. They talk about the state of our schools, high gas prices, unemployment. They also talk about positive things like, "My son is the first to graduate from college, and we're proud of him."

What future goals do you have for your content?

LS: We have a new show called the *World News Magazine Show.* We're also in negotiation with the *Oakland Post* to do a news program. We want to start doing movies. But at the same time, we want to remain in the community because we feel like that's really part of our uniqueness. That's what separates us from all the other African American programming out there.

Leonard, I know that you have invested considerable financial resources to make this dream a reality.

LS: There was a time when even my colleague Chauncey didn't think that this was going to work as a business. He wanted it to be a public access channel. But if we existed as public access, we would just be couriers.

Why does black ownership matter?

CB: Because we have different viewing tastes. The top twenty shows in black households are different from the top twenty shows in white households. You have only three shows that are on both lists. I was sitting in an airport in Kansas City watching CNN doing a report on Earl Lloyd, the first black player in the NBA. Nobody was watching it except me. We need our own channel that speaks our message.

LS: It's part of my ministry that I'm going to continue until the day I die. I'm leaving the legacies for our children so that they can be happy and proud of something that we started.

Why do you think there aren't more African American media owners?

LS: I think there's a lot of mystery to the business, and people kind of shy away from things that they don't know much about. Also, there's a lot of competition, and there are a lot of loopholes.

CB: BET went to white investors. TV One went to white investors. But Leonard has pretty much stayed black entrepreneurial. There's something to that. When a black kid comes up to me in West Oakland, a seven-year-old, and looks at me wearing a tie, and asks, "Are you a businessman?" I say, "Yes, I am a businessman. Don't let the black face convince you that I'm not."

CHAPTER 10

ROBERT D. SHORT, JR.

In his testimony before the U.S. Senate in January of 2003, Robert Short, Jr., now fifty, declared that he was forced to sell his Syracuse radio station, WRDS-FM, in 2000, after just five and a half years on the air. Short, who is the first African American owner of a broadcast radio station in central New York, argues that he was squeezed out of the market largely because of the overwhelming dominance of Clear Channel.

During two visits to upstate New York, I was able to spend time with Robert, his wife, Valary, and their two teenage children, in addition to meeting members of his church, Bethany Baptist, where Short is an organist and his son plays the drums. Pastor Phil Turner is the former sales manager for WRDS, a position he held before joining the ministry. During these visits, it became clear to me that the story of WRDS illustrates how deeply the loss of a single, unifying station can impact a community. Their disappointment was as palpable as their respect and admiration for Short's determination.

It is in this sense that the story of Robert Short is a cornerstone for the entire book. Delving deeply into the aspirations of one man, and the failed mission of one broadcast enterprise, his story brings to life the universal human emotions that might otherwise be missed in the previous stories of relatively rare success.

Those African Americans who succeed in their efforts to own radio and television holdings are the exception to the rule. Far more common is the story of a man such as Robert Short who "did everything right," as he puts it, but still was not able to hold onto his small piece of the American dream.

*   *   *

Let's start at the beginning. Why did you want to own a radio station?

Syracuse was a city without a heartbeat to me. It had no soul. It was all white bread. If you listened to the radio here before I came along, you would wonder, "Is there a black community even in existence?" You'd say, "What's going on in this town?" Oh, they're having a square dance. Okay. You're not against any of those things, but where's the Stone Soul picnic? Where's the Parliament Funkadelic concert? You wouldn't know anything about that. And Syracuse, the city proper, is about 40 percent African American. After we came to the airwaves, there were more concerts for the urban community, for example, because we began to work with promoters. Because if you're Jodesi, you're not going to think of Syracuse first.

Did you feel that it was important to cover issues that impacted the community on WRDS?

We were pretty much an entertainment radio station, as opposed to an issues station. But let me put it to you this way: if our deejay said that the National Council of Negro Women was having their annual Ebony Fashion Fair at the Landmark Theater, the black community now knew about it and they would go down there. You would never know that Ebony was in town if you were relying on the other stations. It wouldn't even be news to them. It would be irrelevant.

You also carried the Tom Joyner Show *via syndication, which is very much issue-oriented programming.*

Yes. Joyner will challenge a company on its hiring practices, or bring up a racial subject that's controversial for the good of his audience.

Why does black ownership matter?

I liken it to black newspapers. If you look at the *New York Times* and the *Amsterdam News* on the same date in history, you might see what President Bush is doing on the front page in one and a story about how test scores in inner-city schools are below average in the other. In the *Amsterdam News*, this becomes the lead story as opposed to the war in Iraq. Not that the other story isn't important, but the black press might bring in someone from the school board and talk about what to do, or offer information about tutoring sources that are available in the community. The kind of stories I really wanted to do were community success stories. Like bringing in the owner of a local business to talk about the services they provide; or talking to a student who was making great accomplishments academically; or if there was a new African American doctor in the community, bringing that person on. It was more community and family oriented. If there was a health fair, we would broadcast from the health center live, telling people to come down to get high blood pressure screening, get tested for diabetes. We also talked about the gun violence program and trying to get guns off the streets.

I noticed, as we were driving, we passed a billboard with the picture of a young black man who was killed here in the neighborhood?

Yeah. That billboard is near Bruce Street and Erie Boulevard. The young man was killed over there and his mother put up the billboard. That would have been a discussion on our station.

What else did you talk about?

Anybody who came to town that was a national figure, we would put them on the air. Yesterday, I was told that the Reverend Jesse Jackson was in town, and he went over to Clear Channel, but he wasn't on the air. There's no way that I would let a Jesse Jackson in my station and not tell the deejay to stop playing music for a few minutes to put him on.

Even though you didn't have the resources to do reporting, it sounds like you were, in fact, offering news and informational programming.

Well, we would look at the *Post-Standard* and if there was a little one-hundred-word article in the back of the local section somewhere about something that was happening in our community, we would emphasize it. So while you were having fun listening to our deejays, they were saying, "By the way, don't forget that the kids' coat drive for Christmas is happening down at Dunbar Center." There was probably no organization in the black community that did not contact the station with events, and hardly anybody was denied, even though very few public service announcements were paid for. Every organization knew that if they faxed it to us, we would read it.

So the community had access to the airwaves.

I used to wonder: were we running the station properly at times? I liked the results we were getting, but I always wondered what made people think that they could just walk in and get on the air. Because our deejays were very community-oriented people, and somebody would stop by and say, "I'm just getting ready to drop this CD, man." And the listener might say, "Why is this guy on the radio?"

But he can't do that at another station, and that's what made us different. We had a guy called "Scratch," and he had his *Scratch Attack Show*. And I would cringe at times because it would be like urban news, and the music would be on in the background, and he'd be saying, "Mr. Mayor, whatcha doin' now? Yeah. We're thinking about trying to get some new jobs in the city. How are you going to help us?" He could do pretty much what he wanted, but it was, from a general manager's standpoint, risky.

You sponsored an annual event that ended up being extremely important to the community.

Unity Day. We brought twelve thousand people together for that.

And members of the community tell me that when the Million Man March took place in 1995, there were large numbers of people from Syracuse who traveled to Washington, DC, specifically because they had heard about it on WRDS.

That's right.

But, primarily, you were a music station. What was wrong with radio offerings in Syracuse prior to WRDS?

In Syracuse, there was a close-knit group of owners, all white males, for the most part, who concluded that this town wasn't big enough in terms of black population to even think about an urban station. Instead, they had block urban programming on Saturday nights, say until ten o'clock, where you could listen to the best in R&B and classic soul or whatever. So if you were black and wanted to hear that kind of music, you'd just wait around until Saturday, and get your tape recorder out and record those three hours.

People recorded them?
You had to. That kept you going for the week. And I would occasionally listen, but I usually refused. I was a single guy at that time, and I was like, "I'm going on a date or something on Saturday night at 7 p.m. I'm not going to be sitting around the house waiting for my favorite song to come on." I said, "I'm not going to let white people tell me when I have to listen to the radio. I will listen to the radio when I want to listen to the radio." My white counterpart doesn't care about radio at seven o'clock on a Saturday night. He's at the movies. He's going out to dinner.

So how does one start the process of owning a radio station?
You have to have the net worth of the money that you're trying to borrow. That way if you fail with your business, the investors can use the collateral, or your assets, to get their money back. But think about it. What is a radio station? It's air. You're selling air. The air belongs to the public. So you're really paying for control and power so that you'll have the right to communicate and influence people. And if you listen to that guy on the radio long enough, after a while you'll be saying, "Hey, he has a point." But they're all his points. No one's asking you for your point. You only get one side.

If you only have one side, what happens to democracy?

It suffers. The power stays in the hands of the people who currently hold it, and the poor little guy never gets a chance to tell his story. Nobody wants to report it, and he or she has no outlet to report it on. So the greater majority decides for you.

What was the station before you bought it?

I built it from the ground up. It was just a sheet of paper from the FCC saying you now have permission.

What happened next?

Well, after you spend a couple hundred thousand dollars to get a permit, you can build. The problem was I didn't have any money left after that.

Okay, let's go back for a minute. You had some competition when you first decided to apply?

Yes. Butch Charles is another African American who used to own a station in this market. He now works for Clear Channel. The city had never had an urban station before. They had a disco station in the '70s. Remember disco?

Sure.

Yeah. So a man named Craig Fox had the first urban station, WOLF-AM. He is not African American, but Butch Charles is, and he ran it. Fox was getting ready to lose the station to the FCC, so he let Butch come in and manage it. They knew I had a pending application before the FCC, which I had filed in 1988. And everybody knew that if I won, I was going urban. I made it known to everybody. I was basically a laughingstock for some people because they thought, "Here's a guy with no broadcast experience who wants to come to this market and do urban, which is the worst format you could pick. And he wants to do it on FM, and he wants to beat us. Good luck." So they laughed, at first. But then they realized that maybe Robert isn't going away. I was still hanging in there for years after filing with the FCC. So around 1991 WOLF decided to go with an urban format, too. So now I had an application pending before the FCC, and Butch Charles had an application before the FCC: two African Americans going after stations and only one of us was bound to win that license. He was just waiting for his license to be approved so that he could drop this rental agreement or whatever he had with Craig Fox and own his own station.

Why didn't Craig Fox put an urban station on earlier? Why did he wait until the FCC was about to take it away from him?

He's a millionaire. This was just something else he owns.

I don't get it.

It's not about the business. It's about power. Why have seven or eight country and western stations in a single market? Because most of the owners are millionaires, and they say, "Hey, I like country music." If color doesn't matter, then let black people own all the radio stations. You'll soon find out that color does matter.

It's about power.

Penn Central, at the beginning of the 1900s, was one of the biggest companies in the United States. But as time went on, people started driving cars and flying on planes, and soon no one was taking the train. All those years, Penn Central thought they were in the train business. They didn't realize they were in the transportation business. It's the same with broadcasters. They forget that their real job is communicating to people and sharing vital information. Like if there's a hurricane coming. You need radio to tell you to take cover. If there is a big event taking place in your town, you want the radio station to tell you about it. But now, even the big, arrogant owners are realizing that there are other sources people can use to get information: the Internet, satellite radio, cable.

Who were your biggest advertisers?

The irony is that my biggest advertiser came when I was selling the station, Coca-Cola. It took five and a half years to get them to start doing business with me.

Why?

Coke wants a demographic of ages twelve to seventeen and seventeen to twenty-four. They want young people. So they were going to the hip hop and modern rock stations. They said we were too adult. Later, we finally broke through the ratings, in their mind, with the young demographic. And when they came on, they came on big time. They placed $30,000 or $40,000. But even as I was dealing with them, I knew I had to sell. I was pretty much done. I was, by that time, a half a million dollars in debt, holding off the bankruptcy lawyers. Even though they might place a $10,000 order right now, and then another one for $15,000 later, it took about $30,000 a month to run the station.

If you had gotten big advertisers all along—
—I wouldn't have had to sell.

That must have been very frustrating for you.
It was extremely frustrating, especially when you do everything that you're supposed to do, and you do it better than your counterpart. If you tell me that ratings are important, I deliver ratings. But I still cannot get the buy. And then they buy from stations with significantly lower ratings than me, and won't even place a little bit of money on my station. It's just plain racism. There's no way around it. You cannot convince me that if you never bought an ad on a station that targets black listeners that you're not racist. I'm not saying that you need to advertise a lot on black radio, but if black people come into your store, then why are your ads in *People* magazine, but not in *Ebony*? Why are your ads on CNN, but not on BET? Why are

they on the country station, the rock station, the news station, and the sports station, but not on the urban station?

Good question.

And it's an obvious answer. There should be some relationship there . . . some ratio between the amount of money you spend with us. But they'll go to a station that gets like a low 0.8 share because it's an affluent demographic, and listeners are highly educated, which advertisers see as better than targeting [what they see as] single moms on welfare or unemployed thugs standing on corners. You remember the Katz Media famous leaked memo that told advertisers they would be getting "suspects" not "prospects."

Yes, and deejay Tom Joyner took them on for that memo. Katz Media President Stu Olds was put in a highly embarrassing position. He quickly vowed to hire more African American sales executives and to increase ad time sold to black radio.

Yes, but if someone advertised on the *Tom Joyner Show*, that money stayed with Disney, who owned ABC, who at the time owned the Joyner show. So on our station, you might hear commercials from J.C. Penney and Gold Bond, and you would think, "Robert must be making a lot of money." But I didn't receive a penny from those commercials because the show was syndicated. J.C. Penney was advertising on Tom Joyner because Tom Joyner is going to put them on two hundred stations at one time. They can buy for the whole country versus dealing with one little local radio station calling them up.

Syndication is good for big corporations.

It's one-stop shopping.

Why don't corporations that advertise with CNN also advertise with BET?

My belief is that they feel they're going to get the money from that community anyway. They know that African Americans like certain products, and that we shop at certain places heavily. Take a store like Wal-Mart. Everybody shops at Wal-Mart. But African Americans *really* shop at Wal-Mart.

And many of the ads you do see have this narrow idea of who we are, for example, the ones with the "sassy" slang.

Right, they don't want a plain-Jane African American. You know, she's got to be either really sexy, or—*with an attitude.*

Right. Honey chil' . . . giiiirl . . . But where is the financial planning commercial with the African American family sitting there talking about college?

You say there are even different pay scales for ads directed at African Americans?

Here are two terms you may be familiar with. One is a decrement factor, and the other is a power ratio. When advertisers go after what they consider highly desirable markets, they apply a power ratio to the rating points that the station delivers. So let's just use mathematical terms to make it clearer. Let's say a show has a five rating and they deliver women very well. They might say, "Wow, we really want to be on that station." So for every rating point you're supposed to get a hundred dollars for the market we're talking about. Theoretically, you'd say one hundred times five, right? So a fair price for a thirty-second spot on that particular radio station should be $500 because you're using the ratings as the common denominator. But someone else may have a station where their rating might also be five, but for whatever reason, the advertiser determines that that particular audience does not have the *qualitative aspects* of listeners you want. That's the decrement ration, which lowers the price. So with both of these, in effect, the same advertiser could be paying $1,000 over here and $140 over there. Now let's take it a step further. An advertiser says I want to buy a hundred spots on one station and maybe twenty on the other. So that person runs a campaign for, let's just say J.C. Penney, and one station might get $1,400 while the other station with the same ratings gets $200,000. Imagine that scenario happening all over. That's just how business is done.

Are you saying the decrement factor always gets applied to black stations?

You always get a decrement if you have a black format.

Do they explain why it's less desirable?

They'll say using qualitative data, such as the household income is lower, educational levels are lower. Things like that.

And how is the power ratio applied?

The perception is that these demographics "deliver," which is really questionable. But if the station actually delivers they'll get double or triple what the advertising agency says they're willing to pay. But it's those kinds of perceptions. And while some of them may be true, they're far too general and subjective to put any real confidence in as your method for doing business.

I see. So with such huge barriers in getting advertising dollars, how do you compete against Clear Channel? In your market they own seven radio stations.

They also own the second largest advertising agency in the country. They own concert venues. If you're going to bring Britney Spears to a theater, that money goes to Clear Channel, too.

They have the whole thing locked down.

And how can you compete? There's no one really managing their stations. They're just sophisticated jukeboxes: computerized music boxes with a few contests and news announcements interjected throughout the day. It's not like there is someone actually there, who's going to speak at your school, or bring you in to talk about issues that are important to you, or somebody that does the school dances. All the kids knew me. My station would come out and do dances for the local elementary school. Those kids weren't even in our demographic, but the parents realized if WRDS was willing to do that, we must really be community based.

Right, it was part of building trust. Let's play devil's advocate. Some people reading this book might say, "Well, there are some major African American owners out there." A few of them are interviewed in this book. So it's not impossible.

Yes, there's Pepe [Pierre] Sutton and Cathy Hughes and Syd Small and people like that. So there was some growth that took place, but not with individual, small owners like myself who only had one or two signals.

You met with Pepe Sutton, who helped you at one point?

Yes, he has invested money in my company. And I was fortunate enough to be able to repay it. We met on numerous occasions with commissioners at the FCC.

How did you become acquainted?

He has a track record of giving back, and I knew that he was fortunate enough to be in a position to help. At the time, around 1997, I think Inner City Broadcasting was possibly the largest black-owned media company in radio, before Radio One took that title. When I was trying to introduce myself to him at a NABOB conference in St. Thomas in the Caribbean, he said, "I know who you are," because there really aren't that many African American–owned stations. So we met, we talked, and I think we had a good connection.

And I think what helped me with Pepe was that he knew that I was very rooted in my community, and that I knew my history. There was some discussion, at one point, and we were laughing as a group about the idea that

African Americans were once considered three-fifths of a human being by a Supreme Court ruling. And Pepe said we were considered two-thirds of a human. And I said, "No, we were three-fifths. No one else corrected Pepe because, you know, he's the most knowledgeable. And then we played bid whist, and I beat him. We must have played all night. . . . I think it's important to ask for help. If a company's doing $50 million a year in revenue, there's a good chance they might have an extra $25,000 or $50,000 to risk on an up-and-coming broadcaster, and that's what Pepe was willing to do.

And yet, you ended up selling your station.

Yes, and you know, some people say, "You should be happy because you made some money." But it wasn't about money for me. It's very frustrating to hear these other guys say, "I have nine stations . . . I have ten stations." And these are guys you were slaughtering in the ratings. Guys you've fallen out of bed beating in the ratings. And they had all the consultants, all the market studies, all the research data, but you were just saying, "I know the people. I know what they want to hear. I don't need a guy looking at a *Billboard* report out of California telling me what to play in Syracuse."

How much did you sell for?

$3.75 million. What I sold the station for, I should have been making in revenue every year. I shouldn't have had to sell. The other guys have already made the millions that they gave me for WRDS.

After selling in 2003, I know you produced a documentary film. Can you talk about that project and why you did it?

Yes. We had a symposium at Syracuse University a few years ago that commemorated the *Brown v. Board of Education* ruling, and there were civil rights journalists from all over the country who came up to be a part of it. While we were there, [producer and radio and television host] George Kilpatrick and myself decided to follow up and do a film about some of the journalists. *Freedom's Call* is a documentary about the role that African American journalists played during the civil rights movement. It was directed by Richard Briar, who is a professor of film at Syracuse University, and produced by George Kilpatrick, who works in public television at WCNY.

What was your role in that production?

I found the money.

What drew you to the project?

If you look at the media today, you have to really question who's out there telling our stories. It's pretty much entertainment, and there's very little news being discussed by African Americans. Everybody's got an opinion, but nobody's telling our stories. That film was a continuation of our commitment to these stories.

Will you receive any compensation for it?

When I first started, I didn't know it was going to cost this much money or this much time. It took an enormous amount of time.

Why didn't you find a job in radio?

Where else do you work? Nobody wants to hire you because they figure you don't need the money. And after you've worked for yourself for so many years, corporate America will not take you back because you're tainted. You've escaped, and you're free. They figure you're too emancipated. I truly believe if I were not African American, having done what I did here in this market, other broadcast companies would say, "We need this guy as a consultant." I mean if I can do what I did with just shaking hands in the community and being myself, imagine what I could do having a financial machine behind me in terms of marketing and promotion.

Would you ever want to be back in the broadcast business as an owner?

Sure. I didn't want to sell the station to begin with.

AFTERWORD

More and more, ordinary people are beginning to realize that monopoly media companies are not serving the public interest. The latest data from the Free Press, the Consumer Federation of America, and the Consumers' Union show that when one media company owns multiple outlets—print and broadcast—in a single market, their total news output falls by as much as twenty-five percent. The news they do manage to produce also tends to be less local in its focus.

African American–owned broadcast stations have fallen dramatically—by seventy percent since 1998. And people of color as a whole, who represent thirty-five percent of the population, own just three and eight percent of all local television and radio stations, respectively.

And yet, Republican FCC chair Kevin Martin continues to lead an aggressive push to further loosen ownership rules and to allow corporate giants to get even bigger while, at the same time, refusing to have his agency provide accurate numbers on minority ownership. At this writing, Martin has attempted to rush a vote through the Federal Communications Commission that, according to the most recent Free Press reports, would allow ninety percent of minority-owned broadcast stations to be targeted by newspaper owners seeking to increase their holdings.

Martin's hasty maneuverings, and the undemocratic procedural manner in which he has run the FCC, have been met with fierce opposition, not only from the two minority Democratic FCC Commissioners—Michael Copps and Jonathan Adelstein—but from Republican commissioner Robert McDowell as well, along with dozens of consumer advocacy and civil rights organizations.

In fact, in early December 2007 Martin became the target of congressional scrutiny as Michigan Democrat John Dingell, chairman of the House Commerce Committee, vowed to investigate Martin's methods, which Dingell and others say amount to a possible "abuse of power."

Michigan Democrat Bart Stupak, chairman of the Subcommittee on Oversight and Investigations, also acknowledged widespread complaints about Martin's attempts to rush through changes without proper review or notification, noting that Martin seems to have worked "to intentionally keep fellow commissioners in the dark."

Martin may be the (deserving) whipping boy this year, but the problem of media ownership is much bigger than one man's myopia, or even one corporation's greed. The problem is about how we, as Americans, see ourselves.

Ask anyone who has ever traveled outside this country, who has sat down for a meal, or played or worked with people from other cultures. Ask anyone who has ever read a newspaper from a foreign city or watched the news in a different language. That person knows that what they are experiencing is the reflection of themselves through another culture's unfamiliar eyes—and it reveals our own beauty in no uncertain terms.

I believe that we, as Americans, are able to see less and less of ourselves and our own unique beauty. How could we, without a clear and accurate reflection to hold up to the light?

December 9, 2007
New York, New York

INDEX